P9-DYJ-500

AN ADVENT DEVOTIONAL

Long-Expected Jesus

Copyright © 2017 by Beacon Hill Press of Kansas City

Beacon Hill Press of Kansas City
PO Box 419527
Kansas City, MO 64141
thefoundrypublishing.com

978-0-8341-3665-6

Printed in the
United States of America

All rights reserved. No part of this publication may be reproduced, stored in a retrieval system, or transmitted in any form or by any means—for example, electronic, photocopy, recording—without the prior written permission of the publisher. The only exception is brief quotations in printed reviews.

Cover Design: Arthur Cherry
Interior Design: Arthur Cherry/Tom Shank

All Scripture quotations, unless indicated, are taken from The *Holy Bible: New International Version*® (NIV®). Copyright © 1973, 1978, 1984, 2011 by Biblica, Inc.™ Used by permission of Zondervan. All rights reserved worldwide. www.zondervan.com.

Scriptures marked (NRSV) are from the *New Revised Standard Version* of the Bible, copyright 1989 by the Division of Christian Education of the National Council of the Churches of Christ in the USA. Used by permission. All rights reserved.

The internet addresses, email addresses, and phone numbers in this book are accurate at the time of publication. They are provided as a resource. Beacon Hill Press of Kansas City does not endorse them or vouch for their content or permanence.

10 9 8 7 6 5 4 3 2 1

WHAT IS ADVENT?

In the early Christian tradition, like its Jewish heritage, seasons of the year were used as opportunities to observe festivals and holidays. These moments of sacred time were set aside to remember and be formed by God's activity in the past in order to prepare for God's activity in the present and into the future. Although the Jewish pattern of keeping time revolved around the exodus from Egypt, the Christian calendar is centered on the life and ministry of Jesus.

The church year begins four Sundays before Christmas—with Advent. This season, often commemorated with the lighting of an Advent wreath, is a time of expectation and hope. Advent not only looks back to the first coming of Jesus but also eagerly and anxiously awaits and calls upon Christ to return quickly. "Come, Lord Jesus Christ. Come and make all things new!" Advent forms a people who can be patient with God's gracious redemption of all things.

In a world where the pace of life continually speeds up, where everything has to come fast, and where attention spans are rapidly declining, it might be wonderfully transformative and counterformative to spend four weeks every year intentionally seeking to be shaped by the patient endurance of God. Advent invites the people of God to endure. It invites them to pray expectantly. It forms people who know that justice and righteousness will not come fully through any human institution or plan but will only break out completely when Christ comes to renew all things.

—Scott Daniels

It might be wonderfully transformative and counterformative to spend four weeks every year intentionally seeking to be shaped by the patient endurance of God.

Long-Expected Jesus

AT A GLANCE

Each **Sunday of Advent** introduces the week's theme:

First Sunday of Advent
He Is Coming
Mark 13:24–37

___

Second Sunday of Advent
He Is Lord
Mark 1:1–8

___

Third Sunday of Advent
He Is Light
John 1:6–8, 19–28

Fourth Sunday of Advent
She Is Chosen
Luke 1:26–38

Christmas Day
He Is Here
Luke 2:1–20

Each **weekly prayer** draws from hymns and psalms.

Come to the Table invites you to gather together in community, preferably on Sundays, for a meal, whether among family or friends. Each Sunday contains a short reflection and discussion questions to share with the group.

While around the table, families or groups can engage in **Family Time**. In addition to the discussion questions are a family activity and suggested memory verse to learn, in order to help bring the weekly theme and scripture to life.

The **daily devotional reflections,** meant to be read throughout the week, have been written by various storytellers, leaders, and pastors.

The **daily readings** of Scripture are based on the Revised Common Lectionary.

IDEA: To help introduce each new scripture for the memory verse challenge, divide a sheet of paper into 9 or 12 pieces.
Then write the scripture out on the pieces so each piece contains a word or two (or three) of the memory verse.
(Don't forget to include the reference!)
Cut out the pieces and lay them face up in order.
Read the verse a couple times together.
Then take turns removing one card and saying the verse again.
Repeat until the verse can be said with few or no cards.

Therefore you do not lack any
spiritual gift as you eagerly wait for
our Lord Jesus Christ to be revealed.
—1 Corinthians 1:7

He Is Coming

WEEKLY PRAYER

Come, thou long-expected Jesus,
born to set thy people free;
from our fears and sins release us;
let us find our rest in thee.
Israel's strength and consolation,
hope of all the earth thou art,
dear desire of every nation,
joy of every longing heart.

Born thy people to deliver,
born a child and yet a King,
born to reign in us forever,
now thy gracious kingdom bring.
By thine own eternal spirit
rule in all our hearts alone;
by thine all-sufficient merit,
raise us to thy glorious throne.

—Charles Wesley

MEMORY VERSE CHALLENGE
If he comes suddenly, do not let him find you sleeping.
What I say to you, I say to everyone: "Watch!"
—**Mark 13:36–37**

DAY 1

Come to the Table

Sunday Scripture Reading:
Mark 13:24–37

Additional Scripture Readings:
**Isaiah 64:1–9; Psalm 80:1–7, 17–19;
1 Corinthians 1:3–9**

---

[35] "Therefore keep watch because you do not know when the
owner of the house will come back—whether in the evening,
or at midnight, or when the rooster crows, or at dawn.
[36] If he comes suddenly, do not let him find you sleeping.
[37] What I say to you, I say to everyone: 'Watch!'"
Therefore you do not lack any spiritual gift as you
—Mark 13:35–37

COME, LORD JESUS

The science fair was one of the most anticipated days of the school year.

We had months to prepare. Parents were invited. Students from other grades were invited. There would be *judges*. The science fair was the culmination of months of hard work and planning. Our teacher had talked about the upcoming fair almost every single week for half the year. We were given guidelines, suggestions, instructions, due dates—everything we needed to prepare adequately.

On the day of the fair, I showed up with something I'd haphazardly thrown together the previous night, and I wasn't fooling anyone who stopped to look at my presentation.

I had plants. No speech. No demonstration. No documented results from a months-long experiment observing and recording their reaction to different kinds of music or the different ways they grow. Not even a poster! Just: plants.

The reason my presentation at the science fair was underwhelming had nothing to do with my lack of knowledge surrounding the assignment, expectations, and deadlines. I had all the information, the resources, and the support I needed. I simply chose not to prepare.

In Mark 13, Jesus is trying to warn the disciples, both about what lies ahead and how they can best prepare for it. There will come a day when the Son of Man will return, and it will be incredible. The kicker? No one knows *when*.

Because we "do not know when that time will come" (Mark 13:33), Jesus encourages his listeners (and us today) to always be ready. We don't prepare for the Lord's return by trying to whip something together at the last minute the night before. Instead, we strive each and every single day, through the power of the Holy Spirit, to love the Lord our God with all

11

our heart, soul, mind, and strength while at the same time striving to love our neighbors as ourselves. Is it always easy? Of course not. Will we fail along the way? Most definitely. But when we take seriously the call and commands of Jesus upon our lives, we posture ourselves in such a way where we can confidently say at any day or hour, "Come, Lord Jesus."

—Jason McPherson

QUESTIONS FOR DISCUSSION OR REFLECTION

What is something for which you have spent time preparing?

What was the benefit of all that hard work and preparation?

In this Advent season, how can we anticipate the coming of Jesus?

How can we *actively* wait?

What does it look like to love the Lord our God with all of our heart, soul, mind, and strength during this season of waiting?

FAMILY TIME

Visit www.adventexperience.com to download and print the first week's family devotional activity sheet. Pass it out to each participating child and help guide them in their response. Once each child has written or decided on their response, hang them in a prominent place in your home as a reminder for the remainder of the Advent season.

If you don't have access to a printer or simply want to design your own, use the question below to get started.

I will prepare for Advent by:

DAY 2

---

¹ In the last days

the mountain of the LORD's temple will
be established
as the highest of the mountains;
it will be exalted above the hills,
and peoples will stream to it.

² Many nations will come and say,

"Come, let us go up to the mountain of
the LORD,
to the temple of the God of Jacob.
He will teach us his ways,
so that we may walk in his paths."
The law will go out from Zion,
the word of the LORD from Jerusalem.

³ He will judge between many peoples
and will settle disputes for strong nations
far and wide.
They will beat their swords into plowshares
and their spears into pruning hooks.
Nation will not take up sword against
nation,
nor will they train for war anymore.
⁴ Everyone will sit under their own vine
and under their own fig tree,
and no one will make them afraid,
for the LORD Almighty has spoken.
⁵ All the nations may walk
in the name of their gods,
but we will walk in the name of the LORD
our God for ever and ever.

—Micah 4:1–5

IN THE LAST DAYS

Even in my earliest memories of her, my grandmother was vocal about her wait for the return of Jesus. She had already lived through the Great Depression, World War II, and Vietnam. She raised eight children and experienced the kind of subsistence living common among poor farmers' wives in the middle of the twentieth century. By the time I got to know her in the 1980s, she was in her late sixties. Her husband, my grandfather, had passed away, her life had become very simple, and she had settled into a pattern of waiting that would characterize her life for the next thirty years. She was a little tired, a little worn, and ready for Jesus to come back for her.

I remember running into her house in between games of tag with my cousins, and there she always sat, rocking ever so slightly in her chair, binding the edges of a quilt. She had grown up Amish and, even after leaving that community, wore a covering for the rest of her life. When she came to the edge of her thread, she gathered a new length, pressing it between her lips. She slipped it through the needle's eye, and then she began to sew again, the needle flashing and clacking against the thimble on her finger.

She often sang quietly,

What a day that will be,
when my Jesus I shall see,
and I look upon his face,
the One who saved me by his grace.
When he takes me by the hand,
and leads me through the promised land,
what a day, glorious day that will be.

She never stopped talking about the last days. Whether it was at the dinner table over roast and potatoes, or out on her porch on a hot summer day shucking corn, her mind constantly came back around to that central hope, that pivotal moment she awaited. She often commented on the strangeness of the times, and when she did, I knew she hoped that her wait was almost over.

When she died, I was not left with an overwhelming sense of loss. Instead, her passing reminded me of the final victory over all things that is yet to come.

On one particular July 4, my cousins and I climbed up on the roof of her house to watch the fireworks. I lay there, the gritty shingles rough under my bare back, scared to death I'd slip off the roof and fall to my death, surrounded by marigolds and petunias. I stared straight up at the fireworks, their explosions reverberating against my tiny ribcage. But always, between the launch and the firework, there was that anticipatory moment of silent waiting. And I thought about my grandmother and wondered what the last days would be like. It frightened me to think about everything I knew and loved coming to an end. I felt very small in those moments, and life seemed tenuous.

As I get older, though, my attitude toward the last days has changed quite a bit. I'm beginning to understand the earnest waiting and expectant attitude my grandmother exhibited. As I witness the drawn-out deaths of people I love, the steady erosions accomplished by age and disappointment, or the horrors that plague our world, I cannot help but feel this strong desire take root inside of me—a desire to see the last days as Micah described them in the third and fourth verses of the fourth chapter: "They will beat their swords into plowshares and their spears into pruning hooks. Nation will not take up sword against nation, nor will they train for war anymore. Everyone will sit under their own vine and under their own fig tree, and no one will make them afraid, for the LORD Almighty has spoken."

Can we even begin to imagine this kind of universe, where worldly power is upended, where war is extinct, where nations no longer prepare for battle but instead seek the mountain of the Lord? Can we even begin to imagine a world where no one is afraid?

These, I think, were the last days my grandmother awaited. She saw a granddaughter die and the resulting pain experienced by her children. She knew the heartache of rebellious offspring. She knew just how lonely a cold winter night could be.

Only a few years ago, my grandmother sat in her armchair, surrounded by her eight children and each of their spouses, her thirty grandchildren, and her great-grandchildren as well. She lay quietly, her mouth slightly open, barely able to talk. But every so often, she whispered that she wanted us all to sing, and sing we did, some of us with tears running down our cheeks.

What a day that will be,
when my Jesus I shall see,
and I look upon his face,
the One who saved me by his grace.
When he takes me by the hand,
and leads me through the promised land,
what a day, glorious day that will be.

18   I think she was surprised to be dying before witnessing those final days here on earth. I think she always expected to see Jesus's return during

her mortal life, to see some miraculous parting of the clouds, to finally hear the trumpet she had heard so much about.

But what we saw happen during that week was no less miraculous. Any swords she carried were beaten into plowshares. Any spears that had been wielded against her in this life were bent into fruitful pruning hooks. In the end, she sat under her own tree of descendants, and she was no longer afraid. In the end, she went up to the mountain of the Lord, the highest of mountains, the one exalted above all other hills.

Strangely enough, when she died, I was not left with an overwhelming sense of loss. Instead, her passing reminded me of the final victory over all things that is yet to come. Now, every Advent season, I think of my grandmother, of her ability to wait patiently for so many years, and I try to do the same.

Maranatha. Come, Lord Jesus.

—Shawn Smucker

DAY 3

Additional Scripture Readings:
Micah 4:6–13 and Revelation 18:1–10

¹ O God, the nations have invaded your inheritance;
they have defiled your holy temple,
they have reduced Jerusalem to rubble.
² They have left the dead bodies of your servants
as food for the birds of the sky,
the flesh of your own people for the animals of the wild.
³ They have poured out blood like water all around Jerusalem,
and there is no one to bury the dead.
⁴ We are objects of contempt to our neighbors,
of scorn and derision to those around us.

⁵ How long, LORD? Will you be angry forever?
How long will your jealousy burn like fire?
⁶ Pour out your wrath on the nations that do not acknowledge you,
on the kingdoms that do not call on your name;
⁷ for they have devoured Jacob and devastated his homeland.

⁸ Do not hold against us the sins of past generations;

may your mercy come quickly to meet us,
for we are in desperate need.
⁹ Help us, God our Savior,
for the glory of your name;
deliver us and forgive our sins
for your name's sake.
¹⁰ Why should the nations say,
"Where is their God?"

Before our eyes, make known among the nations
that you avenge the outpoured blood of your servants.
¹¹ May the groans of the prisoners come before you;
with your strong arm preserve those condemned to die.
¹² Pay back into the laps of our neighbors seven times
the contempt they have hurled at you, Lord.
¹³ Then we your people, the sheep of your pasture,
will praise you forever;
from generation to generation
we will proclaim your praise.

—Psalm 79

IMITATORS OF THE LORD

It's December 1, and I quietly resolve to make this Christmas season less consumer and more communal. I think of the many Christmases past when my heart wanted Jesus but my habits wanted stuff.

The days pass in a blur, and now it's December 26. There has been more purchasing than I planned, more frenetic activities than I hoped for, and less time really sitting with the story and person of Jesus. I've failed again. I wish it could be different. What will it take? I pray, *God, help me to do better next year.*

I want to be the kind of person who doesn't have to choose to settle for less at Christmas because she has already decided that everything done with Jesus equals more. I wish I had the spiritual math down. *Less is more.* Less is really what I want—until I see another family doing this thing or that thing. Jesus and the way of Jesus are what I want—until I feel like I have to keep up for my life to measure up. I want to imitate the love of Jesus and surrender to his love. But, then I don't.

This is the tension I hold in my hands every year during Advent. What do I do with my wandering heart? I don't want to simply *think* that Jesus is Lord. I want to *live* like it, even when I feel like I don't have what it takes.

Have you ever felt this tension? Have you ever feared you don't have what it takes? Have you ever gone through the motions of the Advent season and felt its rich meaning but felt restless in your own skin because you know you've chosen something else over loving Jesus? If you have, it may be a comfort for you to know you're not alone.

Through the storytelling of Paul, we understand that the people of Thessalonica were able to discover that they had what it takes; they were able to experience the good news of Jesus through power, the Holy Spirit, and conviction. The purity of heart we long for doesn't happen all at once but in practice, in transformation, in a place where we surrender perpetually.

You have what it takes too. It may take some time and some training, but you already have what you need. Using what we already have is the part that needs our attention. Your journey into Advent begins with power, not weakness. It begins with a God who doesn't hand out weak words or weak ways. It begins with a God who believed that you were worth Jesus.

You have what it takes. It may take some time and some training, but you already have what you need.

Can you take a moment to let that settle into your thoughts? You and I are worth *Jesus* to God. You and I have the privilege of being called children of God. You and I have access to the same power that was at work in the coming of Jesus Christ into the world. That changes how I feel when I begin to say yes to my heart's longings.

I feel empowered. You should too.

I pray that you feel the power of Jesus in your life this Advent season, that you would know that your heart and your habits can become one. I imagine our hearts and our habits standing on opposite corners in the same city where our decisions live. We stand at the intersection not yet grasping how to follow our hearts without feeling a loss or fear. But we have this power at work within us, the Holy Spirit to guide and connect with us, and we have a conviction that keeps us going.

Be imitators of God, as dearly loved children—because dearly loved children is what we are! Your work can be faithful this Advent, your deeds can be loving, and your heart can be hopeful as you live in the power of God, by the Holy Spirit, with conviction renewed daily by Jesus Christ.

—Brooklyn Lindsey

DAY 6

Today's Scripture Reading:
Psalm 85:1–2, 8–13

Additional Scripture Readings:
Jeremiah 1:4–10 and Acts 11:19–26

---

¹ You, LORD, showed favor to your land;
   you restored the fortunes of Jacob.
² You forgave the iniquity of your people
   and covered all their sins.

⁸ I will listen to what God the LORD says;
he promises peace to his people, his faithful servants—
   but let them not turn to folly.
⁹ Surely his salvation is near those who fear him,
   that his glory may dwell in our land.

¹⁰ Love and faithfulness meet together;
righteousness and peace kiss each other.
¹¹ Faithfulness springs forth from the earth,
and righteousness looks down from heaven.
¹² The LORD will indeed give what is good,
   and our land will yield its harvest.
¹³ Righteousness goes before him
   and prepares the way for his steps.

—Psalm 85:1–2, 8–13

SALVATION IS NEAR

Sometimes all you can do is sing.

It had been a long captivity for God's people. For five decades they waited, they hoped, and they expected. They had been displaced from their home, forcibly removed from the land the Lord promised to their ancestors, and marched off to Babylon, across the same, arid, desert lands where their people had wandered for forty years. With every step away from the promised land, they also took a step away from the promise that had identified them for generations. The Lord told them they were going to be used for divine purposes. The Lord set them apart, gave them a land in which they could prosper and be the kind of people who would demonstrate God's salvation in their very lives. And they lost it all.

Somewhere in the middle of the promise, a silent temptation began to snake its way into their imaginations, quietly calling them away from the pattern of life the Lord had given them, enticing them into a pattern that looked like so many other nations that surrounded them. *Maybe it wouldn't be so bad for us to have a king*, they thought. *Maybe it will actually be good. Maybe it will bring us more protection, safety, security, and prestige than what the Lord has done for us.* I wonder if those were the thoughts on their minds, even as they heard the thunderous sounds of the Babylonian army approaching the walls of Jerusalem.

For fifty long years, they lived in Babylon, a foreign empire that attempted to form them into good Babylonians, wiping away everything that made them distinct. In Babylon, they sat and wept for what had been lost (Psalm 137:1), considered what had happened, wondered where it all went so wrong, and came to terms with their own unfaithfulness and the way they had forsaken the promise. Perhaps that is why, then, when they finally had the opportunity to return to their home and recover the promise, all

33

they could do was sing: "Surely his salvation is near . . . righteousness and peace kiss each other . . . faithfulness springs forth from the earth" (85:9, 10, 11). You can almost hear the poetry on their lips and the joy in their voices.

The kind of people who can sing like that are people who have learned to wait, to hope, and to expect. They are the kind of people who can't help but lift their voices in song when they see salvation dawning. But they are also the kind of people who have probably spent some time humbly remembering what they forgot all those years ago: God is the Lord.

> If we are ever going to be a people of promise who can sing a distinct and joyful salvation song, we must remember who is Lord.

Seasons of waiting, hoping, and expecting often give us time to take an account of those times we have turned away from the pattern of life God has given us, the kind of pattern that sets us free to be a distinct, holy people of promise. We might also remember how we have, at times, turned away from that pattern, charted our own course, and, as a result, lost our precious distinction. Seasons of waiting are good for us to do that kind of remembering. They aren't easy times, but they are good and necessary because God can do gracious and profound work in us during those times, restoring us to the kinds of people who are willing and eager to forsake all the other patterns of life for the one God has offered to us.

The kinds of people who have hoped, waited, and expected are also the kinds of people who can sing when salvation comes. They are the ones who, after returning to the pattern of promise living, can sing, "I will listen to what God the Lord says" (v. 8).

Perhaps we have forsaken the Lord's way. Perhaps we need these times of waiting for God's salvation to draw near; to learn to listen once again. Perhaps we need those seasons to remember that, if we are ever going to be a people of promise who can sing a distinct and joyful salvation song, we must remember who is Lord.

Of course, the salvation that is drawing near is a baby born to peasants. Listening to what God is saying is hearing a Word that was made flesh—lowly, unpretentious, work-callused, wrong-side-of-the-tracks flesh. The salvation that is drawing near is the kingdom he would ultimately go on to establish—the kind of kingdom in which the poor are blessed and the peacemakers will inherit the earth. The salvation that is drawing near is in the pattern of the bloodied cross and empty grave. Something tells me that this kind of salvation is so completely distinct that it will require us to spend some time hoping and waiting for it because it's awfully easy for us to turn toward other patterns. Once we have waited and hoped, though, maybe it could be that there is a song on our lips as we return to God's distinct way: he is the Lord!

I can't help but think about what it would have been like to cross back over that unforgiving and barren wilderness with hearts full of hope and eyes set toward home, to crest the hills that divide the wilderness from the promised land. What might it be like to gaze over the green and fertile lands, for the memories of home and family to come flooding back? For a people who have learned to wait, to hope, and to expect God's salvation—and who have become a more faithful people as a result—I imagine it would be the kind of moment when you couldn't help but sing.

—Timothy R. Gaines

DAY 7

Today's Scripture Reading:
Ezekiel 36:24–28

Additional Scripture Readings:
Psalm 85:1–2, 8–13; Mark 11:27–33

---

[24] For I will take you out of the nations; I will gather you from all the countries and bring you back into your own land. [25] I will sprinkle clean water on you, and you will be clean; I will cleanse you from all your impurities and from all your idols. [26] I will give you a new heart and put a new spirit in you; I will remove from you your heart of stone and give you a heart of flesh. [27] And I will put my Spirit in you and move you to follow my decrees and be careful to keep my laws. [28] Then you will live in the land I gave your ancestors; you will be my people, and I will be your God.

—Ezekiel 36:24–28

I WILL

"I just want to know God's will for my life," said numerous people sitting across my desk, dinner table, or the armrest of my airplane seat. When people tell me this, they usually mean something like, "I want to understand why this tragedy happened to me" or, "I want to know how future events will unfold so I can stop worrying" or, "Please give me a divine justification for the life plan I have already laid out for myself."

When we talk about the will of God we are often trying to understand and even sanctify past, present, and future events. We want some secret decoder ring to fall from the sky so we can decrypt the mysteries of our own lives to find purpose rather than chaos.

The prophet Ezekiel speaks to the ancient Israelite people in the aftermath of great trauma, violence, and displacement. If ever there were a time to find that decoder ring, this would be it. How do they make sense of exile, forced labor, and near destruction of the people of God—the blessed and chosen ones?

In the midst of this confusion and clamor for answers, God speaks, and does so in an unusually direct way: *I will gather. I will cleanse you. I will remake you. I will be your God.* Instead of revealing a divine plan that makes sense of chaos and pain, we hear what God intends to do. Not a play-by-play for each Israelite's individual life—but the activity that reflects the very character and nature of God.

Listen to these words; lean in to hear the voice of God coming to a people desperate to understand the will of God in the wake of trauma and tragedy. Hear the character of God revealed through the activity of God.

I will gather you. You have been scattered to the four winds. You are a tangle of contradictions. Your desires run this way and then that way. Consistency, reliability, faithfulness—these are not in your vocabulary, let alone your character. I would say that you are lost, but you don't seem to want to be found. Oh, people of God, how far you have strayed, and you can't find your way back. So, *I will gather you.*

My will is to gather and not to scatter you. My desire is for your wholeness and fullness. The scattering of your ancestors may have been typical in a sinful world, but I can create what this world cannot produce. I long to see you put back together, reconciled to me and to one another. I am for you, all of you. I will see the fullness of my people gathered together to worship my name.

I will cleanse you. There is no shortage of idols among you. You have seen the way of the world, and you lust day and night for more: more power, more satisfaction, more strength, more wealth, more influence. Your heart is so full of all this garbage that there is no room for me. You love your rituals, but each time you go to wash, you come out filthier than before. I can't even recognize you under all the layers of sin. So, *I will cleanse you.*

My will is to cleanse you and not to scorn you. I desire more than ritual; I want to wash off all the years of disobedience, resentment, bitterness, hate, fear, betrayal—to cleanse you like a newborn child so I can stare into the face of my beloved creation.

I will remake you. I formed you from the dust of the ground, but you wanted more than these humble beginnings. I gave you a heart of flesh. How did it calcify so quickly? Sin has no power to create, but it does destroy; it destroys what I have made. It is destroying you, my people, aiming right for the heart I placed in your chest. You cannot dodge the fatal wound that has shattered your stone-cold heart. So, *I will remake you.*

My will is for creation, not destruction. I hung the moon and told Orion where to fasten his belt. I fashioned you with my own two hands: the Word and the Spirit. Because I desire life and not death, I will give you a new heart. But I won't stop there. I will breathe my Spirit into your lifeless body that was made from dust and will return to dust again—and even then, I will always be your Creator, eternally making all things new.

When we talk about the will of God we are often trying to understand and even sanctify past, present, and future events.

I will be your God. I gave you my name. I gave you the name only angels had sung. I placed it over you to bear that name for all the world to see. But now the nations laugh when they hear my name. Let's be clear: I am not a joke. Yet you have made me a fool among the nations. Perhaps I *am* a fool to give my name to a people who put it on and take it off each time the weather changes. So, I will be the fool once again: *I will be your God.*

My will is for the glory of my name. You are not very glorious, so I will give you a name that is. My desire is that the nations might see that my glory is not in their power. My glory is foolishness to the world, but they will laugh for only a little longer because I am coming to be your God.

I will stop at nothing to gather you. I will spare nothing to cleanse you. I will never cease re-creating you. This is my will for you. And I will do it. Just watch. I will give my name, the name above all names, to one like you. You will call him Jesus. Every tongue in heaven and on earth will call him Lord. He will gather, cleanse, and remake you because he will be God, in a body made of dust. He will be your God, so that you can be my people. Whenever it is hard to see my will in the midst of this scattered, dirty, hardened world, look at him. He is my final "I will," and he is for you.

—Shawna Songer Gaines

Righteousness goes before him and
prepares the way for his steps.
—Psalm 85:13

SECOND SUNDAY OF ADVENT

He Is Lord

WEEKLY PRAYER

Lord, make me an instrument of your peace.
Where there is hatred, let me sow love;
where there is injury, pardon;
where there is doubt, faith;
where there is despair, hope;
where there is darkness, light;
where there is sadness, joy.

O, divine Master,
grant that I may not so much seek
to be consoled as to console;
to be understood as to understand;
to be loved, as to love.
For it is in giving that we receive,
it is in pardoning that we are pardoned,
and it is in dying that we are born to eternal life.

Amen.

—St. Francis of Assisi

MEMORY VERSE CHALLENGE

And this was his message: "After me comes the one more
powerful than I, the straps of whose sandals I am not
worthy to stoop down and untie. I baptize you with water,
but he will baptize you with the Holy Spirit."
—Mark 1:7–8

Come to the Table

Sunday Scripture Reading:
Mark 1:1–8

Additional Scripture Readings:
**Isaiah 40:1–11; Psalm 85:1–2, 8–13;
2 Peter 3:8–15a**

---

[1] The beginning of the good news about Jesus the Messiah, the Son of God, [2] as it is written in Isaiah the prophet:

"I will send my messenger ahead of you,
 who will prepare your way"—
[3] "a voice of one calling in the wilderness,
 'Prepare the way for the Lord,
 make straight paths for him.'"

[4] And so John the Baptist appeared in the wilderness, preaching a baptism of repentance for the forgiveness of sins. [5] The whole Judean countryside and all the people of Jerusalem went out to him. Confessing their sins, they were baptized by him in the Jordan River. [6] John wore clothing made of camel's hair, with a leather belt around his waist, and he ate locusts and wild honey. [7] And this was his message: "After me comes the one more powerful than I, the straps of whose sandals I am not worthy to stoop down and untie. [8] I baptize you with water, but he will baptize you with the Holy Spirit."

—Mark 1:1–8

LONG-EXPECTED JESUS

They knew he was coming. From one generation to the next, the stories had been passed down as a constant reminder that they were not a forgotten people. The prophets spoke of a Messiah who would come, God's Chosen One, who would reign forever—the King of Kings and Lord of Lords. So they waited and waited, retelling the stories of Abraham, Moses, Isaiah, and all the rest—hoping the Messiah would come in their lifetime and they would be able to see the long-awaited Savior with their own eyes.

Then a strange man arrived and began baptizing and preaching repentance and forgiveness of sins. Could he be the Messiah they waited for? Could he be the one of whom the prophets had spoken? The baptizer quickly put these claims to rest. He asserted, in no uncertain terms, that he was not the Messiah, was not Elijah, was not even a prophet. Yet still the people came. They came to be baptized, and they came to hear him preach. John assured them, "After me comes the one more powerful than I, the straps of whose sandals I am not worthy to stoop down and untie" (Mark 1:7).

If they chose in that moment to believe that what John the Baptist said was truth, then the Messiah they had been waiting so long for *was* coming—and they might even live to see him! The words of John the Baptist carried hope. After centuries of waiting and centuries of prophecies, their patience and anticipation would at last be rewarded. Theirs was no longer a story that hinged on the past or the ancient prophets. Here in their midst was a man who claimed that the Messiah, the Lord of Lords, would soon arrive.

—Rachel McPherson

QUESTIONS FOR DISCUSSION OR REFLECTION

In what way(s) did John the Baptist prepare the way for Jesus?

In the Gospel of Mark, John the Baptist said, "After me comes the one more powerful than I, the straps of whose sandals I am not worthy to stoop down and untie." Why was it important for John the Baptist to say this? What was John trying to clarify for those whom he was baptizing in the name of repentance?

How can we be messengers for Jesus in our lives and in how we interact with those around us?

FAMILY TIME

Visit www.adventexperience.com to download and print the second family devotional activity sheet. Pass it out to each participating child and help guide them in their response. Hang the responses in a prominent place in your home as a reminder for the remainder of the Advent season.

If you don't have access to a printer or simply want to design your own, use the questions below to get started.

Jesus was important to John the Baptist. He spent his entire life preparing people for when Jesus would come.

What are some ways you can show your friends and family that Jesus is important to you?

How can our actions and the choices we make today help make a way for Jesus?

DAY 9

Today's Scripture Reading:
Acts 2:36–42

Additional Scripture Readings:
Psalm 27; Isaiah 26:7–15

---

[36] "Therefore let all Israel be assured of this: God has made this Jesus, whom you crucified, both Lord and Messiah."

[37] When the people heard this, they were cut to the heart and said to Peter and the other apostles, "Brothers, what shall we do?"

[38] Peter replied, "Repent and be baptized, every one of you, in the name of Jesus Christ for the forgiveness of your sins. And you will receive the gift of the Holy Spirit. [39] The promise is for you and your children and for all who are far off—for all whom the Lord our God will call."

[40] With many other words he warned them; and he pleaded with them, "Save yourselves from this corrupt generation." [41] Those who accepted his message were baptized, and about three thousand were added to their number that day.

[42] They devoted themselves to the apostles' teaching and to fellowship, to the breaking of bread and to prayer.

—Acts 2:36–42

THIS JESUS, WHOM YOU CRUCIFIED

Advent is the coming of light in the midst of darkness. We gather as church communities, we light candles, we sing songs of joy that the light has come. It's a joyful, warm image, and we hold onto it with all the strength we possess. Pastors preach it as the arrival of a small flame in a dark room. It's a tailor-made season for those who are waiting—those who have been beaten down and trodden upon, and who hope for someone to come to their defense. It's for the lonely, the silenced, and the broken. Advent, at its core, is a season of hope for those who dare not hope. It's a season of expectation for those who have been relentlessly let down. It's good news for those desperately in need of good news.

However, there's another side to this coin. Over the course of our lives, we pack our inner closets and basements full of the stuff we hope to forget. In the shadowy corners, we stuff our wounds, our addictions, our imperfections, our failures, our shame, our embarrassing behavior, our resentments, and our prejudices. We all have a basement inside ourselves—and we all hate what resides there.

Even though we spend so much time dutifully and openly praying for light to come, it has an annoying tendency to illuminate even our most carefully hidden places. Light bleeds into closets and through floorboards, exposing the basements of our souls. When the light threatens to illuminate those shadowy spaces, we typically do anything we can to extinguish it. We humans will do nearly anything to ensure this illumination doesn't happen.

This coming of light is what got Jesus killed. Throughout his life, the teachings and rebukes of Jesus repeatedly exposed the shadowy spaces of the powerful and the common alike. It revealed their idols. It exposed

49

their anger and called the violent to repent. The light came and exposed humanity for who and what it was. In the glow of that light, humanity stood exposed and witnessed the full humiliation that only truth can reveal. The light exposed humanity, and therefore, humanity hated the light. The crowd responded the only way it knew how. It killed Jesus.

Peter named the darkness. Peter called the crowd in Acts 2 to account when he declared, "God has made this Jesus, whom you crucified, both Lord and Messiah" (v. 36). *The light came*, Peter said, *and you killed him*.

Peter knew a thing or two about shadows being exposed. He was the man who, when the chips were down and it mattered the most, denied Jesus three times. He was a man who was shown to be a coward in the face of resistance. Yet here Peter was, speaking rebuke to the very crowd he was once afraid to confront. Peter experienced the worst of himself, had the shame of his darkness revealed—and came out the other side.

Peter's story reveals a great truth about the light. To experience the light—to find its brightness exposing our darkness—is a humiliating experience. We'd rather nobody know about the worst of our past or the ugliest of our present, which is why most resist the light's piercing gaze. We struggle to believe God can examine our whole selves and still love us as we are.

Peter must have felt this way. In those days after Jesus's death, the weight of his failure must have hung heavy around his neck. And yet, from the shore, came a voice. Around a campfire, questions were asked. "Peter, do you love me?" "Feed my sheep." Peter learned on that shore the truth about the light.

Yes, the light reveals our darkness. Yes, the light brings to the surface decades of shame. Yes, it's the most painful act imaginable to stand naked before a holy God. And yet, in the midst of our nakedness, in the presence of our filth and the laundry list of our failings, we realize that we stand not in the presence of a wrathful, judgmental deity but under the loving gaze of a father.

"Peter, do you love me?" Jesus asked. "Feed my sheep" (see John 21:15–17).

This redemption would not have been possible had Peter not experienced his darkness. The boldness in his words would have been absent had he not stood in the light of the Father and been found wanting. Peter's sermon in Acts 2 was not the sermon of a man who had it all together. They were the words of a man who realized the power had never been his in the first place. They were the words of a man who was standing in the light and proclaiming the kingdom of God from that light.

We struggle to believe God can examine our whole selves and still love us as we are.

After the sermon, the crowd had two options. They could reject Peter's rebuke and snub the call to repentance. They could do as they did with Jesus and call for his head. Their shame could move them to silence the voice calling them to account for their sins.

Or . . .

The crowd could accept this call as true, they could repent of their sins, they could believe in the lordship of Christ and be receptive to the work of the Holy Spirit. They could be transformed.

The crowd chose the second. Immediately upon Peter's call for repentance, the crowd felt their hearts pierced. They felt their consciences disturbed. In this moment, as a response to the bold proclamation of the man who denied Jesus three times, the crowd came face to face with who they were and what they had done. And they repented. The Greek word used here is μετανοια (*metanoia*), and it means to change one's heart—literally, change direction.

The invitation of the light is not to stand in perpetual darkness, judgment, and shame. Rather, the invitation is to be exposed, forgiven, and redeemed. This radical redemption characterized the radical lives of the early church. In the wake of such forgiveness, all concerns with possessions, power, or privilege fall by the wayside.

The light has come, and it invites us to be changed. Will we let it in?

—Michael R. Palmer

DAY 10

Today's Scripture Reading:
Psalm 27

Additional Scripture Readings:
Isaiah 4:2–6 and Acts 11:1–18

---

¹ The Lord is my light and my salvation—
whom shall I fear?
The Lord is the stronghold of my life—
of whom shall I be afraid?
² When the wicked advance against me
to devour me,
it is my enemies and my foes
who will stumble and fall.
³ Though an army besiege me,
my heart will not fear;
though war break out against me,
even then I will be confident.

⁴ One thing I ask from the Lord,
this only do I seek:
that I may dwell in the house of the Lord
all the days of my life,
to gaze on the beauty of the Lord
and to seek him in his temple.
⁵ For in the day of trouble
he will keep me safe in his dwelling;
he will hide me in the shelter of his sacred tent
and set me high upon a rock.

⁶ Then my head will be exalted
above the enemies who surround me;
at his sacred tent I will sacrifice with shouts of joy;
I will sing and make music to the Lord.

⁷ Hear my voice when I call, Lord;
be merciful to me and answer me.
⁸ My heart says of you, "Seek his face!"
Your face, Lord, I will seek.
⁹ Do not hide your face from me,
do not turn your servant away in anger;
you have been my helper.
Do not reject me or forsake me,
God my Savior.
¹⁰ Though my father and mother forsake me,
the Lord will receive me.
¹¹ Teach me your way, Lord;
lead me in a straight path
because of my oppressors.
¹² Do not turn me over to the desire of my foes,
for false witnesses rise up against me,
spouting malicious accusations.

¹³ I remain confident of this:
I will see the goodness of the Lord
in the land of the living.
¹⁴ Wait for the Lord;
be strong and take heart
and wait for the Lord.

—Psalm 27

WHOM SHALL I FEAR?

As a teenager, I once told my mom, "If Christians actually believed what we say we believe about the gospel, we'd be flocking to the most dangerous places on earth. We would be the first ones present in the midst of crisis and war." These many years later, I still believe that to be true, but many of us can't imagine fleeing *toward* war-torn areas or places of extreme poverty. In fact, many of us can't even envision ourselves running toward those of our neighbors who are *like* us, let alone people who are as different from us as they could possibly be. Certainly missionaries embody this type of lifestyle, but in the realm of Christianity, career missionaries comprise their own minority category. What keeps the rest of us from moving out of our homes and into the world? More often than not the answer is fear.

We have all experienced moments of fear in our lives. Sometimes— many times—those moments descend upon us without warning. One moment we're blissfully content, and the next moment, the phone rings and we're gripped with anxiety surrounding how our lives could change. We fear seemingly simple things, like darkness, heights, and spiders, but we also can be consumed by greater, less tangible fears.

When we are honest with ourselves, we can recognize these more abstract yet ever-present fears. Our fear of others—people we don't know, who are different from us, who look different from us or believe differently than we do. Our fear for our children—that they will be injured or that they will not end up being who we hope they will be. Our fear for our health and well-being—as we Google, despite our better judgment, that spot on our arm that just doesn't seem to go away. Our fear of change—that life is moving so quickly we cannot keep up.

Our fear of putting ourselves out there to try new things, to have new experiences—because something might go terribly wrong.

There are as many fears as there are people, and these fears can be suffocating. If we allow them, our fears can take over and cause tremendous damage in our lives and in the lives of others. Fear can lead to missing out on great opportunities to be all that God is calling us to be, but it can also lead to much darker things. Fear can lead us to racism, where we constantly question those who look different from us. Eventually, the fear or suspicion of others can lead us into hate. Fear can lead to rejection of the oppressed because we are so concerned with our own well-being that we disregard the well-being of others. Fear has led to countless wars in this world, as we've sought to secure boundaries and scapegoat others. Fear often reveals the worst parts of ourselves—the parts that push people away, turn would-be friends into enemies, and keep us locked out of living up to our God-given potential.

If we allow them, our fears can take over and cause tremendous damage in our lives and in the lives of others.

It's no wonder that "Do not be afraid" is such an integral part of the Christmas message. Mary was told not to be afraid when she learned she would conceive the Son of God. Joseph was told not to be afraid to take Mary as his wife. The shepherds were told not to fear when the declaration was made to them of the Messiah's birth. All of these people were very much human, and all of their lives were about to change drastically—yet they were told not to fear this news and not to fear the future but, rather, to embrace the Messiah.

This message of "do not be afraid" is not restricted only to Advent or Christmas, though. It's a theme throughout all of Scripture, and in Psalm 27, we see a strong imperative against fear. Though there were lists of reasons to be afraid even then, the psalmist declared: "The LORD is the stronghold of my life—of whom shall I be afraid?" (v. 1).

This psalm is a reminder that we do not need to live in fear. We do not need to fear enemies—perceived or real—because God is with us. We do not need to fear abandonment—because God has adopted us as sons and daughters. We do not need to fear any myriad of dangers—because God is faithful. We can follow God boldly. We can embrace whatever God is calling us to because, as the incarnation illustrates to us, God walks with us through it all.

This Advent, what are you afraid of? What fears are holding you back from moving forward in faith? As we prepare our hearts to celebrate the coming of Christ, how can you intentionally remove fear from your heart and trust in Jesus more? What big and bold adventure is God calling you to that can only be achieved by shedding fear and living in faith?

May God help us walk boldly into situations from which others flee. May God empower us to sow love, kindness, and compassion in a world that desperately needs them. May the Holy Spirit stir our hearts to live into our callings, however big or impossible they may seem. May we walk forward out of fear and into faith, knowing that Jesus walks with us every step of the way.

—**Robbie Cansler**

DAY 11

5 In the time of Herod king of Judea there was a priest named Zechariah, who belonged to the priestly division of Abijah; his wife Elizabeth was also a descendant of Aaron. 6 Both of them were righteous in the sight of God, observing all the Lord's commands and decrees blamelessly. 7 But they were childless because Elizabeth was not able to conceive, and they were both very old.

8 Once when Zechariah's division was on duty and he was serving as priest before God, 9 he was chosen by lot, according to the custom of the priesthood, to go into the temple of the Lord and burn incense. 10 And when the time for the burning of incense came, all the assembled worshipers were praying outside.

11 Then an angel of the Lord appeared to him, standing at the right side of the altar of incense. 12 When Zechariah saw him, he was startled and was gripped with fear. 13 But the angel said to him: "Do not be afraid, Zechariah; your prayer has been heard. Your wife Elizabeth will bear you a son, and you are to call him John. 14 He will be a joy and delight to you, and many will rejoice because of his birth, 15 for he will be great in the sight of the Lord. He is never to take wine or other fermented drink, and he will be filled with the Holy Spirit even before he is born. 16 He will bring back many of the people of Israel to the Lord their God. 17 And he will go on before the Lord, in the spirit and power of Elijah, to turn the hearts of the parents to their children and the disobedient to the wisdom of the righteous—to make ready a people prepared for the Lord."

—Luke 1:5–17

A PEOPLE PREPARED FOR THE LORD

Luke introduces us to Zechariah and Elizabeth, a couple who struggled with the darkness of barrenness. Though they enjoyed a beautiful marriage, they had not become parents as expected. Suddenly we discover that they were chosen to play a special role in the coming of the Messiah. The light that would dawn for the whole world shone first on them, for they were told they would have a son who would serve as a prophetic voice.

Zechariah and Elizabeth were not ordinary characters in their day, but they were specifically chosen because of their heritage and their faithfulness in the midst of disappointment. They were both from the priestly line of Aaron. Priests were required to marry virgins of Israelite birth, but a priest did not always marry a woman from a priestly family. To marry the daughter of a priest was considered significant, and for Elizabeth to be not only the daughter of a priest but also an actual descendant of Aaron was remarkable.

Augustine, in *Sermon 293*, brings an interesting perspective to this passage:

> The church observes the birth of John as in some way sacred . . . When we celebrate John's, we also celebrate Christ's [birth]. . . John is born of an old woman who is barren. Christ is born of a young woman who is a virgin. Barrenness gives birth to John, virginity to Christ. The normal and proper age of parents was lacking with the birth of John. No marital embrace occurred for the birth of Christ. The former is announced in the declaration of the angel. With the angel's annunciation the latter is

conceived. That John will be born is not believed, and his father is silenced. That Christ will be born is believed, and he is conceived by faith. First of all faith makes its entry into the heart of the virgin, and there follows fruitfulness in the mother's womb.

Zechariah and Elizabeth were faithful in their service to God. Luke made note that they lived "observing all the Lord's commands and decrees blamelessly" (1:6). They were a remnant embodying the best of Old Testament law, and they would now serve as a bridge between the old and the new. The gospel of Jesus Christ is not in conflict with Old Testament law but becomes the fulfillment of the law as revealed in Christ. A slight glimpse of daylight was breaking at the horizon.

We may not be called to give birth to a divine messenger, but we are called to carry the divine message.

For both Elizabeth and Mary, conception was truly a miracle and each one especially significant as a symbol to women. All women suffered from the time of Eve's sin and—very specifically, as prophesied—in the area of childbirth. Pain was associated with childbirth, not just because of the delivery process but even in the very desire to have children. Children were the hope of the future, the hope of old age. Not having children might mean that a woman would be cast aside. A husband could divorce a wife for not producing children.

The darkness of Elizabeth's barrenness was great because barrenness was often seen as a punishment from God for sin. Yet Elizabeth and Zechariah were viewed in their community as righteous people who had lived exemplary lives even when faced with disappointment. As a result, God was able to use them—just as God had used other barren couples in the past—to bless them with a child who was called to fulfill a divine task. Early readers of Luke's Gospel would remember women like Sarah—barren and well beyond her childbearing years—and recognize that only divine intervention would make pregnancy possible. Elizabeth's son would be born to fulfill God's purposes and to announce the arrival of light into the world.

This message of good news was not just for Elizabeth; it was God reaching out to daughters and sons in an incredibly loving and holy touch of restoration, for Elizabeth's barrenness was symbolic of the barrenness of God's people. They had not been producing spiritual children in the way God intended. Now there would be a new era, and her child was to be the voice of one calling in the wilderness, bringing light to make way for the Lord! Israel was about to become fruitful again as the barren woman gave birth to a prophetic voice pointing to the Savior.

God is still in the business of shining light into the darkness of our world. We may not be called to give birth to a divine messenger, but we are called to carry the divine message. There is hope when we feel barren. Spiritual barrenness has a cure that comes from the loving touch of the Holy Spirit in our lives. God's children can again bear fruit when the miraculous and majestic power of the Holy Spirit does its work. We are to desire to know the Messiah in such an intimate way that he becomes a part of our very being. Then we carry the divine messenger into a dark, hurting world that needs a light.

When we find ourselves in that dark space, wondering whether there is any hope, the one who dwells in the presence of God comes and ministers to us at our point of need. Elizabeth responded in obedience to the call, and God's promise was fulfilled. We are called to obedience in all things to the will of the Father, who will provide the fruit. Barrenness and virginity have never been an obstacle to the power of the Holy Spirit, bringing God's people to a place where they could again be healthy, fruitful, and multiply.

Advent is a season of hope and anticipation. Many people think they await the gifts under the tree. We await the Light who will take us from our barrenness and use us as messengers of hope. Think about what you do today and how you can live faithfully, carrying light into a dark world.

—Carla Sunberg

DAY 12

Today's Scripture Reading:
Philippians 3:7–11

Additional Scripture Readings:
Psalm 126 and Habakkuk 2:1–5

7 But whatever were gains to me I now consider loss for the sake of Christ. 8 What is more, I consider everything a loss because of the surpassing worth of knowing Christ Jesus my Lord, for whose sake I have lost all things. I consider them garbage, that I may gain Christ 9 and be found in him, not having a righteousness of my own that comes from the law, but that which is through faith in Christ—the righteousness that comes from God on the basis of faith. 10 I want to know Christ—yes, to know the power of his resurrection and participation in his sufferings, becoming like him in his death, 11 and so, somehow, attaining to the resurrection from the dead.

—Philippians 3:7–11

THAT I MAY GAIN CHRIST

In Philippians 3, we discover a driven man. Saul of Tarsus (who had become Paul by the time he wrote Philippians) was passionate about everything he did. Whatever he set out to accomplish, he did with all of his heart. But his tenacity and determination were not what kept Saul from experiencing the light of Christ; rather, his focus and motivation blinded him to the truth.

In our highly individualized society, looking after yourself and your own interests is encouraged and affirmed. It is natural for us to think of ourselves. And there is nothing wrong with assuming personal responsibility or setting and achieving personal goals—but it will never lead you to the light of Christ.

In Philippians 3:5–6, Paul highlighted his credentials as well as his achievements in order to make a point. When he was still called Saul, his Jewish-religious life was all about doing the right things. He was driven to generate and preserve God's light for a dark world. Now, mind you, there's nothing wrong with doing good deeds. The passionate pursuit of righteousness is a commendable attribute. But it can blind you to the light of Christ if it becomes your driving motivation.

Everything changed for Saul one day when he was confronted with the light of Christ while pursuing his driven agenda (see Acts 9). That head-on collision with Jesus transformed him from a driven man to a called man. From that moment on he would become Christ-focused, not self-focused, an example of which is clearly demonstrated in Philippians 3. In verses 7–10, Paul mentioned the name of Christ no fewer than five times. Jesus wasn't just an addendum to Paul's life. Jesus *was* Paul's life. And as a result, his motivation changed as well. Instead of measuring his worth

63

by his credentials and achievements, Paul discovered his value in being identified with Jesus. Instead of being driven to generate and preserve the light of God, he simply *reflected* the light in his quest to become "found in him" (v. 9).

Driven people sacrifice everything in order to succeed, but called people sacrifice everything in order to be faithful to the One who calls.

During my formative years, I was driven to do good things. And, if asked about my motivation, I would have said I was doing those things for God. But I was actually driven to please others. I was driven by personal achievement. My focus was on my own success. I tried to prove to others and to myself that I was a good person or an excellent student or an accomplished musician or a great communicator, and the list goes on. Only when I quit trying to impress God with my achievements and humbly accepted God's call did I begin to understand what Paul wrote about in these verses.

Advent is a good season for personal reflection. Paul offered a couple of tests to help us determine whether we are living our lives as driven people or as called people.

First, he testified that driven people are primarily motivated by winning, achieving, and succeeding. Called people, on the other hand, are primarily motivated by their love for Jesus. It's all about strengthening the relationship with Jesus. If, as Paul wrote in verse 9, there is nothing more important than to "be found in him," this means Jesus becomes your closest friend and confidant. You go everywhere with him. You do everything with him. You would never intentionally do anything to damage that trust or hinder that relationship. Even a driven life of righteousness, if it is not a called life, will eventually leave a person unfulfilled and empty. A life of fulfillment can only be found in "the righteousness that comes from God on the basis of faith [in Christ]" (v. 9). When you find your identity in the Light of the world, you will reflect his light to the world.

Second, driven people sacrifice everything in order to succeed, but called people sacrifice everything in order to be faithful to the One who calls. In verse 10 Paul testified, "I want to know Christ—yes, to know the power of his resurrection . . ." Driven Christians stop right there. That's the ultimate success. But *called* Christians seek faithfulness over success. And that desire compelled Paul to add, "I want to know . . . participation in his sufferings, becoming like him in his death" (v. 10). Sharing in the suffering of Jesus is the key to true faithfulness. That's where the light of Christ is best seen in us.

If this Advent brings you hardship and suffering, it may be that you are best positioned to reflect the light of Christ to those around you who are living in the darkness of their sin. As you become "found in him," may the light of Christ more clearly shine through you so others can experience the light as well.

—Mark Fuller

DAY 13

Today's Scripture Reading:
Psalm 126

Additional Scripture Readings:
Habakkuk 3:2–6 and Philippians 3:12–16

———

¹ When the Lord restored the fortunes
of Zion,
we were like those who dreamed.
² Our mouths were filled with laughter,
our tongues with songs of joy.
Then it was said among the nations,
"The Lord has done great things
for them."
³ The Lord has done great things for us,
and we are filled with joy.

⁴ Restore our fortunes, Lord,
like streams in the Negev.
⁵ Those who sow with tears
will reap with songs of joy.
⁶ Those who go out weeping,
carrying seed to sow,
will return with songs of joy,
carrying sheaves with them.

—Psalm 126

THOSE WHO SOW WITH TEARS

In the movie *Christmas Vacation,* Clark Griswold is a caricature of a family man full of over-the-top Christmas cheer. He loves all the Yuletide festivities and romanticizes what it should be like for loved ones to come together on the brightest of all holidays. Clark's outdoor decorations have since become legendary, covering nearly every square inch of his exterior property in gaudy lighting. It makes for a beautiful mess, combining good intentions with poor execution and resulting in a strain on the local power grid. Even though he is likely unaware, Clark is actually paying appropriate homage to the birth of Christ with all of those lights.

The psalmist once spoke words foretelling the coming of the Messiah. He spoke about the great joy and laughter the people would experience as God brought them out of their captivity and exile. Abiding in joy brings light to a world awash in darkness. Think with me for a moment about the benefits of light.

Light aids life. The first words God spoke in creation were, "Let there be light" (see Genesis 1). Before anything else in the world was created, God started with light. Life cannot exist without light.

Light empowers awareness. Without light, we'd walk blindly in a world filled with obstacles and pitfalls and traps just waiting to ensnare us.

Light offers clarity. Without light, I can't tell blue from green. Without light, I wouldn't be able to see the diversity in all of God's good creation. Darkness brings a measure of conformity, whereas light illuminates nuance, difference, and diversity.

Light encourages growth. Plants count on light in order to participate in the ordered systems God set out for them, like photosynthesis, growth, and rebirth.

We celebrate the birth of Jesus because we are a people who lean toward darkness and captivity. We want to do our own thing, regardless of the consequences. And, sadly, we are rarely self-aware enough to identify our own areas of need—not to mention our lack of ability to empathize with the real needs of others.

Luckily for us, Jesus as Light of the World brings us out of the darkness of our captivity, our chains, our exile—both what we create for ourselves and what is created for us. Jesus is the Light, and he is a true cause for legitimate Christmas cheer. What we've sown in tears, Jesus reaps for us in songs of joy. Let's consider the same benefits of light but insert the name of Jesus.

Light and liberation have come in the person of Jesus Christ.

Jesus *is* life. In the Bible, it's easy to notice that Jesus was always changing people everywhere he went. He gave life to a few physically dead people, sure, but he also gave life to those with broken bodies, buried hopes, and blinding disabilities. And it's the same today. Anyone who invites Jesus into their lives at any moment walks directly out of the darkness of exile and into the marvelous and joyful light of Jesus.

Jesus empowers awareness. When I communicate with Jesus personally, I am confronted with ultimate truth, which guides me into the best life I can have—one that's filled with laughter and songs of joy, just like the psalmist said.

Jesus offers clarity. Walking with Jesus allows me to appreciate the diversity in all of creation, including other people I might normally not enjoy. Jesus brings joy to my heart and lightness to my life that fears and worry cannot destroy.

Jesus encourages growth. Jesus was a tremendous teacher who expected his biblical followers to actually *do* the things he asked of them. He would show and tell, and then he expected them to go and do. Jesus grows us by challenging our comfort zones—especially during our periods of captivity and exile and darkness—so that, when we are liberated by the Light, we can become smaller versions of his light for a world that desperately needs the warmth.

Light and liberation have come in the person of Jesus Christ. How do we respond to this Savior who transforms our sorrows into a glorious celebration? We can choose to exult in the freedom from exile that Jesus brings, or we can continue to live with the consequences of darkness and captivity. The choice is ours.

—**Brett Rickey**

DAY 14

Today's Scripture Reading:
Matthew 21:28–32

Additional Scripture Readings:
Psalm 126 and Habakkuk 3:13–19

---

²⁸ "What do you think? There was a man who had two sons. He went to the first and said, 'Son, go and work today in the vineyard.'

²⁹ "'I will not,' he answered, but later he changed his mind and went.

³⁰ "Then the father went to the other son and said the same thing. He answered, 'I will, sir,' but he did not go.

³¹ "Which of the two did what his father wanted?"

"The first," they answered.

Jesus said to them, "Truly I tell you, the tax collectors and the prostitutes are entering the kingdom of God ahead of you. ³² For John came to you to show you the way of righteousness, and you did not believe him, but the tax collectors and the prostitutes did. And even after you saw this, you did not repent and believe him.

—Matthew 21:28–32

THE WAY OF RIGHTEOUSNESS

Matthew was an amazing and strategic writer. His Gospel is filled with themes and sub-themes that have deep significance. But finding the significance can sometimes be a challenge. A passage read in isolation can seem to have a different meaning than when it is read in the larger context of the Gospel of Matthew.

The parable of the two sons, found only in Matthew, is one of those unique and sometimes puzzling passages. Scholars often struggle with the fact that there are two or more versions of the parable. The order of the addresses to the two sons by the father (or vineyard owner) is reversed in some early versions of Matthew. The response of those who are being questioned by Jesus can seem uncertain or ambiguous in that case. However, the parable must be seen in its context in this particular phase of the ministry of Jesus as recorded by Matthew. The chief priests and elders of the people were plotting how they might at least discredit him or, at most, kill and destroy him. The growing tension and their murderous intent would not have been lost on early readers of this Gospel.

What are we to make of these two sons? Remember: there is a context to the parable! To read the story in isolation is to miss the point. The twenty-first chapter of Matthew is filled with stories of conflict and challenge. From Jesus's triumphal entry into Jerusalem, all the way through to the question about Jesus's authority, the tension was building.

As Matthew unfolded the story of Jesus it became obvious that Jesus was by now treading on dangerous ground. The authorities were frustrated and annoyed that they were unable to simply call a halt to his effectiveness in healing the blind and the broken. The crowds hailed him "son of David," and he stormed through the temple grounds, overturning tables and driving the merchants away. The next day he was back, teaching in the temple courts. You can almost feel the anger in their voices when they challenged him: "By what authority are you doing these things . . . And who gave you this authority?" (21:23).

The "authorities" were obviously frustrated at their distinct lack of authority. Faced with an authority they were forced to acknowledge yet confused about where that authority came from, they came face to face with a reality they could see but could not change.

Matthew strategically arranged the entire flow of his Gospel story in such a way that this passage brought Jesus into even more visible, tension-producing conflict with the chief priests and the elders. In the passage just prior to the parable of the two sons, Jesus asked them about John's baptism. They had heard John's message and seen him baptize the people who came to him. The outcasts came, confessing their sins and submitting to baptism by this rugged prophet, repenting and turning their lives around. Among those who came to hear his message were Pharisees and Sadducees, religious leaders, many of them perhaps officers of the temple, elders, teachers of the law. John's most scathing message was directed toward those religious leaders. "Repent," he demanded of them. "Bear fruit that demonstrates your repentance! Turn your life around!" (see Matthew 3).

Words alone are never enough.

It is imperative to read Matthew 21:28–32 with an active memory and a discerning mind. Jesus did not waver when the religious leaders, seeking to demonstrate their own authority, challenged his. Rather, in telling the intriguing story of the two sons, Jesus demonstrated their utter lack of spiritual and moral authority.

The parable of the two sons reached into the depths of human sin and rebellion. The first son, given a reasonable and expected request by his father to go work in the vineyard—the source of the family's income and welfare—stubbornly refused to go. One can only imagine the questions that ran through the minds of those who heard the story: *What was that son thinking? Why would anyone refuse such a request?* But, for some reason, that son later had a change of heart and went to the vineyard.

The second son, quickly and with the expected response, agreed to go to the vineyard and work. However, his words were meaningless. He simply did not fulfill his promise.

In challenging the religious leaders' evaluation of the ministry of John the Baptist, Jesus forced them to deal with their own response to that ministry. Who responded to John's ministry? Who humbly confessed their sins and turned their lives around? It was, in fact, the people whose response mimicked that of the first son. These were people who had, by their very lives and attitudes, shunned the Old Testament law. However, when confronted with their utter need for God's forgiveness, these people—the "tax collectors and the prostitutes"—acknowledged their sins. They repented. Their lives were changed. The Pharisees and Sadducees— religious leaders who were supposedly bent on protecting the law— probably said, "Oh, sure. I don't mind being baptized. It will probably be a good thing to demonstrate my willingness to identify with the people. Hey, let's all get baptized!"

One consistent emphasis for Matthew throughout his Gospel is the absolute necessity of obedient trust. Words alone are never enough. Life, for followers of John the Baptist and later Jesus, must be a demonstration of repentance, of obedient trust, and of grateful response to the wonder of God's gracious act of forgiveness.

Advent is the season of preparation. It is a time of getting ready for the coming of Christ, whether a celebration of his first coming or a meaningfully engaged anticipation of his return. We have to prepare. But the preparation entails far more than decorations on a tree. We must "prepare him room," make place for obedient trust, and live in joyous anticipation of his coming again!

Joy to the world!

—**Jesse C Middendorf**

The Spirit of the Sovereign L<small>ORD</small> is on me, because the L<small>ORD</small> has anointed me to proclaim good news to the poor. He has sent me to bind up the brokenhearted, to proclaim freedom for the captives and release from darkness for the prisoners.
—Isaiah 61:1

THIRD SUNDAY OF ADVENT

He Is Light

WEEKLY PRAYER

Christ with me
Christ before me
Christ behind me
Christ in me
Christ beneath me
Christ above me
Christ on my right
Christ on my left
Christ when I lie down
Christ when I sit down
Christ when I arise
Christ in the heart of everyone who thinks of me
Christ in the mouth of everyone who speaks of me
Christ in every eye that sees me
Christ in every ear that hears me

I arise today
through a mighty strength, the invocation of the Trinity,
through belief in the Threeness,
through confession of the Oneness
of the Creator of creation.

MEMORY VERSE CHALLENGE
There was a man sent from God whose name was John.
He came as a witness to testify concerning that light,
so that through him all might believe.
—**John 1:6–7**

Come to the Table

Sunday Scripture Reading:
John 1:6–8, 19–28

Additional Scripture Readings:
**Isaiah 61:1–4, 8–11; Psalm 126;
1 Thessalonians 5:16–24**

———

[6] There was a man sent from God whose name was John. [7] He came as a witness to testify concerning that light, so that through him all might believe. [8] He himself was not the light; he came only as a witness to the light.
—John 1:6–8

THE LIGHT OF JESUS

In every single generation throughout history there has been an understood relationship between light and hope. For the weary sailor who has been lost at sea for days, a glimpse of light in the distance promises safety. For the young child who wakes up suddenly from a nightmare— fearing what might be under the bed or in the closet—light brings comfort. In many religious traditions and worship settings, the simple act of lighting a candle can symbolize divine presence and life. We only have to read to the third verse of Genesis to see the significant and foundational role that light played in creation: "And God said, 'Let there be light, and there was light." By its very nature, light can guide us, lead us, help us, give us life, and show us the truth.

The first-century Roman world knew what it was like to be guided by the light. In the evening, when the fire burned down and slowly turned to ash, the town became dark. When the sun set, the workday was over. When the sun rose, a new day began. Light, and the absence of light, determined the rhythm and tempo of daily life.

When the Scriptures refer to Jesus as the Light, the symbolism and imagery are incredibly powerful. As the Light, he desires to lead and guide us into all truth. As the Light, he calls us to listen to and follow him. As the Light, he desires to expose and expel any darkness that might reside within us. The Light calls us to turn away from the darkness of our sin. And as the Light, he desires to birth new life within us. When we welcome Christ—the true Light—into our lives, we are made new.

—Jason McPherson

QUESTIONS FOR DISCUSSION OR REFLECTION .

What are some other examples of ways that light can bring hope?

How has Jesus been a light to you or people you know?

How can we show the light of Jesus to others?

In what ways can we make sure we hear Jesus's voice in our lives? What are some ways that help us listen?

FAMILY TIME

Visit www.adventexperience.com to download and print the third family devotional activity sheet. Pass it out to each participating child and help guide them in coloring, drawing, or writing their response. Hang them in a prominent place in your home as a reminder for the remainder of the Advent season.

If you don't have access to a printer or simply want to design your own, use the prompt below to get started.

The light of Jesus makes me think of:

DAY 16

Today's Scripture Reading:
Ephesians 6:10–17

Additional Scripture Readings:
Psalm 125 and 1 Kings 18:1–18

---

[10] Finally, be strong in the Lord and in his mighty power. [11] Put on the full armor of God, so that you can take your stand against the devil's schemes. [12] For our struggle is not against flesh and blood, but against the rulers, against the authorities, against the powers of this dark world and against the spiritual forces of evil in the heavenly realms. [13] Therefore put on the full armor of God, so that when the day of evil comes, you may be able to stand your ground, and after you have done everything, to stand. [14] Stand firm then, with the belt of truth buckled around your waist, with the breastplate of righteousness in place, [15] and with your feet fitted with the readiness that comes from the gospel of peace. [16] In addition to all this, take up the shield of faith, with which you can extinguish all the flaming arrows of the evil one. [17] Take the helmet of salvation and the sword of the Spirit, which is the word of God.

—Ephesians 6:10–17

IN THE STRENGTH OF THE LORD

It started as a small tremor in his hand. I first noticed it from my chair in the front row, where the flute section sat, when he tried to hold his hand behind his back while he spoke. He tried to keep it under control as he conducted us in practices and performances, but it was no use. One day, he finally told us what was going on: he'd been diagnosed with Parkinson's disease. Only a couple of years later, he was additionally diagnosed with ALS, also called Lou Gehrig's disease. Both are incurable.

Our band director was one of the most loved professors on our college campus. From that distinguished position as professor and performer, he began a very slow, very painful, and very public journey toward death. I didn't have the privilege of conversing in depth with him, but I imagine there were times when his suffering was immense and he asked God the questions we all confront at times: "Why, Lord? Won't you bring healing and end my suffering?"

We don't have to look far to find examples of suffering or injustice. The news shows us all kinds of things happening in our world. We might not even have to turn on the television to see it; maybe the suffering is a very personal kind.

The people of Israel were not strangers to suffering and injustice. Their land was full of it. First, it came to them from the outside—from the overpowering nation of Assyria and an advancing military threat. Oppression from conquering nations brought enormous demands on people's way of life as they were required to provide food, livestock, clothing, or whatever else might be desired by soldiers as they passed through the land—sometimes even the lives of their strongest family members.

But the suffering and injustice began to come from inside Israel as well. As their own rulers became intimidated by the world's superpowers, these kings and prophets forgot that their primary responsibility was to God and God's people. Instead, they began reflecting this culture of intimidation and power by coveting wealth (Micah 2:2) and neglecting the poor (3:5).

And of course, as is so often the way of God, the answer of God —the Word of God—didn't come as one would expect.

The nation of Israel found itself in a dark time. We can almost hear their hearts crying out for peace: "O Lord, haven't your people suffered enough under the oppression of these foreign powers? Haven't we had more than our share of corrupt kings and deceitful prophets? Please, Lord, make it end. When will you bring your justice and peace?"

Perhaps at first they couldn't hear God's answer to their cries. It approached quietly, from ever so discreet a place as the little town of Bethlehem. And of course, as is so often the way of God, the answer of God—the Word of God—didn't come as one would expect. It came as one who was small and vulnerable and poor. None of those things would be the world's choosing for a Savior. But that didn't matter because even one who is small and poor by the world's standards is, through the Spirit of God, strong and majestic. As our passage declares in verse 4: "He will stand and shepherd his flock in the strength of the LORD."

It was the promise to Israel, the answer to their suffering, for this One of Peace to come. This one who did not seem to be anything impressive would come and stand in the midst of the suffering and give nourishment and strength to those who needed it so desperately.

It is the promise to us as well. Although this One of Peace has already come, we also wait for him to come again. And as we anticipate him, we allow ourselves to be used in the same way he was.

After several years, our beloved professor found himself unable to direct a concert band. He couldn't play his trumpet. He could not lecture or teach. He did not seem to be able to do much of anything. But somehow, he managed to get on a plane and make his way to an African country, to a small village of children who were unexpectedly delighted to receive musical instruments that they perhaps had never seen before. And they even received some lessons! How could that happen? How could someone so weak, so overcome by disease, provide education, hope, and joy to those in need? It echoes the promise from ancient days: he will stand and shepherd his flock in the strength of the Lord.

Where is there suffering? Where is there injustice? As we wait for the One of Peace to come again, would we let ourselves—in our weakness and insufficiency—be filled with the strength of the Lord? Would we let ourselves be used to feed and strengthen others? May we stand in the midst of the suffering flock as ambassadors of peace, that our lives would reflect the majesty of the name of the Lord our God.

—Deanna Hayden

DAY 5

Today's Scripture Reading:
1 Thessalonians 1:2–10

Additional Scripture Readings:
Psalm 85:1–2, 8–13; Hosea 6:1–6

---

² We always thank God for all of you and continually mention you in our prayers. ³ We remember before our God and Father your work produced by faith, your labor prompted by love, and your endurance inspired by hope in our Lord Jesus Christ.

⁴ For we know, brothers and sisters loved by God, that he has chosen you, ⁵ because our gospel came to you not simply with words but also with power, with the Holy Spirit and deep conviction. You know how we lived among you for your sake. ⁶ You became imitators of us and of the Lord, for you welcomed the message in the midst of severe suffering with the joy given by the Holy Spirit. ⁷ And so you became a model to all the believers in Macedonia and Achaia. ⁸ The Lord's message rang out from you not only in Macedonia and Achaia— your faith in God has become known everywhere. Therefore we do not need to say anything about it, ⁹ for they themselves report what kind of reception you gave us. They tell how you turned to God from idols to serve the living and true God, ¹⁰ and to wait for his Son from heaven, whom he raised from the dead—Jesus, who rescues us from the coming wrath.

—1 Thessalonians 1:2–10

Today's Scripture Reading:
Micah 5:1-5a

Additional Scripture Readings:
Psalm 79 and Luke 21:34-38

¹ Marshal your troops now, city of
troops,
for a siege is laid against us.
They will strike Israel's ruler
on the cheek with a rod.

² "But you, Bethlehem Ephrathah,
though you are small among the clans
of Judah,
out of you will come for me
one who will be ruler over Israel,
whose origins are from of old,
from ancient times."

³ Therefore Israel will be abandoned
until the time when she who is in labor
bears a son,
and the rest of his brothers return
to join the Israelites.

⁴ He will stand and shepherd his flock
in the strength of the LORD,
in the majesty of the name of the LORD his
God.
And they will live securely, for then his
greatness
will reach to the ends of the earth.

⁵ And he will be our peace
when the Assyrians invade our land
and march through our fortresses.

—Micah 5:1-5a

There's a tradition in my twelve-step recovery that asks me to make a list of my character defects. And then, most terrifyingly, I am to share that list with a sponsor or pastor or counselor, or basically anyone who won't run screaming from the room. My list included anger. Inferiority. Pride. Pain and chaos from years back. These are not unique sins but ones that we, the whole human race, share. Is it possible, then, that generational sin is just basic pain and pride, trickling down from mother to son, and so on, because we first observed from Adam and Eve how to pass the buck?

Not long ago, at a meeting, I found myself sounding like the psalmist with a litany of worries and fears. "Why did I ever allow my drinking to take over? Didn't I know this would affect my boys? I can't forgive myself for that. What if they become like me?"

Then someone said, "Did you ever think, Dana, that your addiction—and your recovery—are also a gift to them? That it might be a wonderful thing for them to 'become like you'? Your kids will grow up with a mom who understands surrender. They will grow up understanding who is truly in charge of your life. They get to grow up with a miracle as a mom.'"

In matters of faith, it doesn't get worse. It just gets real. The psalmist does the simplest thing. He asks a lot of questions. He faces the mess. And then he begs for mercy. I beg for mercy too, on a daily basis. And, as the end of Psalm 79 shows us hope and glory, I realize generations don't carry only sin. We can carry redemption and praise and hard-won strength too. Onward and forever. Thank you, Lord Jesus.

—**Dana Bowman**

23

son flopping to the floor in soap-operatic despair when he could not find his shoe (under the couch, within five-inch range). As I stood over him, I realized that all of these histrionics were basically . . . me. Except for the flopping, I don't flop. It's too hard on my back.

But wait, it gets worse.

We seem adrift. We have forgotten our inheritance with Christ. Watch thirty minutes of the news and you'll see that rubble is all around. And then we have our sweet little responsibilities—our children—living amidst all that rubble. Won't some of the mess we've created tip over onto our offspring? It's enough to make any parent want to run for the hills. But these would be quiet, tidy hills with no arguing or politics or R ratings.

In matters of faith, it doesn't get worse. It just gets real.

I got sober when my boys were babies, and the years since have been a journey toward grace and forgiveness. But I also know the sharp bitterness of truly understanding generational sin. I am an alcoholic. My father is also an alcoholic in recovery. My brother died from alcoholism. On and on, the sad song plays out. The rhythm of this disease beats strongly in our family.

I am grateful that my children don't have to see the wreckage of active alcoholism in my life. But I still have rubble. It's no longer in a bottle, but it's piled all around. My rubble is anxiety. It's fear. It's lack of faith. And with every news headline, it shifts and grows, and I am in desperate need.

We are all in desperate need.

FROM GENERATION TO GENERATION

I never really understood generational sin. It's mentioned in the Old Testament, and I would read about it and categorize it as one of those Really Serious Old Testament Topics. It seemed grim and overly dramatic, like a curse on the countryside from a wicked stepmother. Reading about it made me grateful for the New Testament, with all its happy Jesus stories.

I know. My biblical knowledge was severely lacking. Let's face it: for the longest time God and I were at a Little Golden Books level. This all changed, however, when I got sober. It was when I was my weakest, trapped in my addiction, that God was strong. And isn't this always the way? When I was at the end of myself, I clung to a beginning with Christ. And then I saw him as part of the Old Testament, together with the New Testament, and the story of all of life. Glory to God.

But honestly, the concept of generational sin still overwhelmed me. I always figured I had enough problems on my own. I didn't need a bunch of ancestral mess-ups for added flair.

But that's where my children come in. They are *my* next generation in the flesh, after all, wreaking daily havoc and cuteness right in front of me. A six-year-old and an eight-year-old have illuminated for me love, sacrifice, and relational living on a deeper level than I ever comprehended.

They crack things open, children do. They have no idea.

If sin were its own novel in my childless life, it became encyclopedic with my kids in tow. And I don't just mean my kids' sinfulness. I mean my own wickedness, to which my children are a constant, sticky audience. Just as my boys constantly reenact *Star Wars* light-saber duels, they also mimic me, but in this case, imitation is not flattery. I recently observed my eldest

THE FULL ARMOR OF GOD

Somewhere in the thick fog of early motherhood, I stopped praying.
I tried, while wiping down countertops with a damp rag. I tried, while
lying down by the glow of a nightlight with a wriggling infant, or while
driving to or from my part-time, overnight job. But there was a relentless
pace to life that left me constantly exhausted, and these attempts at prayer
prattled on like stream-of-consciousness thoughts that more or less strung
themselves together like a chain of pleas for life to settle down; for the
busyness of my life in grad school—with three little ones and a part-time
job and a stack of bills that wouldn't relent—to just get easier.

In the wildness of my unfocused heart, I wandered. I wordlessly shouted
one-word prayers for patience, for peace, for gentleness—as I struggled
to potty-train my two-year-old or when my husband was working late,
again. But I wasn't actively seeking patience, peace, or gentleness. Outside
of church and small groups, my Scripture reading was limited to whatever
alert popped up on my phone's Bible app—if I chose to open it. If there
was time.

One Sunday, my son came out from a lesson with a picture that he handed
to me in a flurry of four-year-old excitement. I looked down at a cartoon
of a soldier, colorfully scribbled all over. I recognized it well from my own
childhood in Sunday school classrooms—knights and soldiers, armed with
shields and swords, shining helmets, elaborate breastplates. Like scenes
from medieval mythology, we learned about the armor of God.

It was never a passage that particularly resonated with me—the military
analogy lost on my younger self, the lessons reading like instructions for
war, for a fight—when I was doodling flowers and hearts on the corners
of notebook pages. Imagery of soldiers drawing swords of the Spirit or

buckling truth around their waist—it all just circled around in my brain as though I was never actually the intended audience.

Until motherhood. During one bitterly cold winter, my three-year-old stood in front of our door, fuzzy hat pulled down over her ears, three layers of shirts, pink waterproof boots—but no pants. Her eyes were fixed down at her fingers, fumbling to button the round, wooden buttons all by herself so she could go and join her siblings in the snow outside.

"Can I help you?" I asked, but she resisted, stomped her feet, and told me she could button without any help. "I meant with your pants," I explained, and went to get her some regular pants and snow pants and gloves to prepare her for the January afternoon. "You can't go outside without pants. You'll freeze."

Putting on the armor of God is not about winning a battle.

Antsy to catch up with her siblings, she huffed and harrumphed as I made her take the time to pull on each layer. The thickest socks, the warmest gloves, the heavy jacket. Tugging the final zipper up to her soft chin and tucking wisps of hair away from her face, I nodded, satisfied in the knowledge that she would be protected from the cold, the wet, and the wind. "Now," I said, smiling, "you're ready." And in that moment, crouched down eye to eye with a winterproof three-year-old I was about to send off into a snowy afternoon, the Sunday school lesson somehow came into focus in my heart.

She could have gone outside, emboldened and excited but pantsless and without her heavy jacket. The snow would have burned her bare skin pink, her boots would have filled with icy slush, and her toes would have ached until they turned numb. Left alone to the elements, she would not have survived—which is why we took the time to protect her from the elements.

There, kneeling in front of my daughter, my heart flashed back to the cartoonish visions of knights and soldiers dressed for battle, with righteousness, truth, the sword of the Spirit, and so on. For the first time, I saw them as not simply preparing to fight in a war but as being protected by a loving God. Putting on the armor of God is not about winning a battle. It's about being able to stand secure and safe, even in the wilderness of this life, with its swirling temptations and deceptions and distractions, even amid all the elements that would have us bend or break.

I could continue to go out into the wilderness of my life, woefully unprepared, muttering half-hearted prayers and without spending any time refilling my spiritual well. Or I could make time to protect myself— not as a chore, not as one more obligation in a busy life, but as a necessity. Just as I wouldn't ever let my daughter go out unprotected into the snow, I need to remind myself daily to spend time putting on the protections God has provided.

I don't want to be a soldier. I've never wanted to see a battlefield. But life sometimes *is* one, and I want to rely on a strength that is greater than my own. I don't want to be lulled away or bent by the distractions of busyness or anything else in this world. I want to stand, strong and safe.

—Melanie Haney

DAY 17

Today's Scripture Reading:
2 Kings 2:9–22

Additional Scripture Readings:
Psalm 125 and Acts 3:17–4:4

---

⁹ When they had crossed, Elijah said to Elisha, "Tell me, what can I do for you before I am taken from you?"

"Let me inherit a double portion of your spirit," Elisha replied.

¹⁰ "You have asked a difficult thing," Elijah said, "yet if you see me when I am taken from you, it will be yours—otherwise, it will not."

¹¹ As they were walking along and talking together, suddenly a chariot of fire and horses of fire appeared and separated the two of them, and Elijah went up to heaven in a whirlwind. ¹² Elisha saw this and cried out, "My father! My father! The chariots and horsemen of Israel!" And Elisha saw him no more. Then he took hold of his garment and tore it in two.

¹³ Elisha then picked up Elijah's cloak that had fallen from him and went back and stood on the bank of the Jordan. ¹⁴ He took the cloak that had fallen from Elijah and struck the water with it. "Where now is the LORD, the God of Elijah?" he asked. When he struck the water, it divided to the right and to the left, and he crossed over.

¹⁵ The company of the prophets from Jericho, who were watching, said, "The spirit of Elijah is resting on Elisha." And they went to meet him and bowed to the ground before him. ¹⁶ "Look," they said, "we your servants have fifty able men. Let them go and look for your master. Perhaps the Spirit of the LORD has picked him up and set him down on some mountain or in some valley."

"No," Elisha replied, "do not send them."

¹⁷ But they persisted until he was too embarrassed to refuse. So he said, "Send them." And they sent fifty men, who searched for three days but did not find him. ¹⁸ When they returned to Elisha, who was staying in Jericho, he said to them, "Didn't I tell you not to go?"

¹⁹ The people of the city said to Elisha, "Look, our lord, this town is well situated, as you can see, but the water is bad and the land is unproductive."

²⁰ "Bring me a new bowl," he said, "and put salt in it." So they brought it to him.

²¹ Then he went out to the spring and threw the salt into it, saying, "This is what the LORD says: 'I have healed this water. Never again will it cause death or make the land unproductive.'"

²² And the water has remained pure to this day, according to the word Elisha had spoken.

—2 Kings 2:9–22

DIDN'T I TELL YOU?

The water stopped flowing as Elisha, an untested and unknown young man, stepped into the now dry riverbed. The familiarity of having crossed this river before was eclipsed by the sense of the unknown; the last time he came this way, Elijah had parted the waters and they walked over together. Now, he walked alone.

The cloak on his shoulders didn't fit quite right. Perhaps he'd grow into it one day, but today it felt too large, both in the way it hung from his frame and in what it represented for his people. When he and Elijah, the elder prophet who had been God's spokesman for a generation, had crossed this river the first time, it had been from the known goodness of the promised land into the wilderness territory beyond the Jordan. As he returned, though, it seemed as if he were stepping into a new wilderness of the unknown. He was going to speak for God now; he was going to wear the cloak of the prophet, and this was most certainly the "difficult thing" Elijah had promised it would be (2 Kings 2:10).

As they watched him return from the wilderness alone, the other prophets recognized the spirit that was upon him. "The spirit of Elijah is resting on Elisha," they said to one another, bowing in respect (v. 15). Not a moment had passed before their amazement turned to concern: *What happened to Elijah? What happened to the man who spoke God's word to us all these years? We need to find him,* they said to Elisha, pointing out that fifty of their strongest men would certainly be up to the task. Then Elisha spoke as a prophet, and his first words were none too comforting. "No, do not send them" (v. 16).

This wasn't just a logistical command. It was prophetic guidance for a people who were beginning to feel lost. If you've ever suffered the loss of someone who tied your family together for a generation, you probably know what this would have been like, and you can probably identify with their instinct. "We need to find him," they probably said to one another, their desperation growing, "because, without him, how else will we go on as the people of God?"

They knew nothing of this young man Elisha, except that the spirit of Elijah now rested on him. At least they were able to see that much. Still, their instinct was to head out and search for what they'd known previously. Everything they had known before—a prophet they appreciated, a face they recognized, a voice they knew—instilled in them the kind of trust we place in those who have faithfully gone before us, speaking God's word to us for years.

Of course, they saw that it was the same spirit of Elijah that now rested upon Elisha, but how could God possibly speak through this young unknown? They couldn't help but set out in search of Elijah, to try to recover what they had known. The young prophet was only beginning to find his voice when he said to them, "No, don't go searching," a prophetic word to trust in the faithful consistency of God, doing the same redemptive thing in a new and unexpected way.

That is part of Advent's mystery and challenge. We hope, we wait, we expect. But what if what we are waiting for is something God does that we didn't expect? In this passage Elisha, the young prophet who was chosen and anointed to speak God's word to the people, reminds me of another young person who was chosen and anointed to bring God's Word forth to the world. I hear Elisha's "Let me inherit a double portion of your spirit" (v. 9) begin to harmonize with Mary's song in Luke 1:46–55 and her own response to the message she received: "The Holy Spirit will come on you, and the power of the Most High will overshadow you" (v. 35). No one expected Mary to be part of God's redemptive work. An unlikely girl giving birth to a very unexpected baby was a departure from what anyone was looking for. But it was the same Spirit on Mary who had spoken order into chaos in the beginning, and now God was doing the same work of redemption in a very unexpected way.

Perhaps, as Elisha slipped Elijah's cloak around his shoulders, straightened his young back, and turned to face the Jordan, Mary's own question could have been on his lips: "How can this be?" (Luke 1:34, NRSV). How can it be that God's own Spirit would act in this way, choosing this unlikely person and, in so doing, opting to redeem the world in this utterly different way? Perhaps this is where the challenging and discordant question begins to pierce the beautiful harmony of Elisha and Mary's song: *Will I trust God's redemption, even it if looks different from what I expected?*

But what if what we are waiting for is something God does that we didn't expect?

The significance of this question is pressing for us during Advent. Advent—that season of hope and anticipation—if nothing else, is a time of waiting for God to do something. But what if God does something we didn't expect? What if God answers our hopes and expectations in an unexpected way? Will we have the eyes to see and the ears to hear the redemptive song God is singing, or will we turn away from the music in search of what we knew in times past?

Perhaps Jesus came singing Elisha's prophetic song: "Don't go searching for what had been, but see how the Spirit has faithfully given an unexpected gift of salvation!" (see Luke 4:14–19). After all, who expected that a peasant child born in a barn could be what God's Spirit would give us? Our God has a long history of doing the same redemptive thing in unexpected ways—though, even as the ways may change, the Spirit does not. Maybe the thing we are hoping for is something we couldn't possibly expect.

—Timothy R. Gaines

DAY 18

Today's Scripture Reading:
Mark 9:9–13

Additional Scripture Readings:
Psalm 125 and Malachi 3:16–4:6

---

⁹ As they were coming down the mountain, Jesus gave them orders not to tell anyone what they had seen until the Son of Man had risen from the dead. ¹⁰ They kept the matter to themselves, discussing what "rising from the dead" meant.

¹¹ And they asked him, "Why do the teachers of the law say that Elijah must come first?"

¹² Jesus replied, "To be sure, Elijah does come first, and restores all things. Why then is it written that the Son of Man must suffer much and be rejected? ¹³ But I tell you, Elijah has come, and they have done to him everything they wished, just as it is written about him."

—Mark 9:9–13

COMING DOWN THE MOUNTAIN

Mountaintop experiences are a regular feature in the story of God's relationship with God's people. God called Moses to the mountain, and there Moses heard the voice of the Lord. Elijah, when he was running for his life, went to the mountain, and God met him in a special way—not with spectacular demonstration but with "a sound of sheer silence" (1 Kings 19:12, NRSV).

The people who raised me in the faith talked about mountaintop experiences. These were sacred moments, graced awareness of the majesty and love of God. I have experienced some of these mountaintop spiritual moments, and they are indeed wonderful. There's just one problem. We eventually come down the mountain. We don't get to live up there all of the time. We come back to everyday, mundane, Monday-morning life. Moses came down. Elijah came down. And Jesus, Peter, James, and John came down.

As mountaintop moments go, it doesn't get much better than Mark 9:2–8. It's the story of Jesus being transfigured in the presence of these disciples so that "his clothes became dazzling white" (v. 3) and they heard the voice of God. No wonder Peter wanted to set up tents and just stay there. The mountaintop is wonderful.

Eventually the disciples had to go back down the mountain, back into real life. They were going back to the crowds and the problems. Like us, perhaps, they began to stress over everyday life because they had been to the top of the mountain. Coming down can be depressing. One may begin to question the validity of the experience as the emotions fade. We can nearly see these disciples with their drooping shoulders and low-hanging chins as they trudged back down the mountain.

But there's something we cannot miss in this passage in Mark 9. Yes, they did have to come down the mountain and face the problems awaiting them. However, between the account of the transfiguration and coming down the mountain, we get verse 8: "Suddenly when they looked around, they saw no one with them any more, but only Jesus." Jesus was still there! The vision was over and the cloud gone. The mountaintop moment had ended, but Jesus remained. Yes, these disciples came down from their mountaintop experience, but Jesus came with them!

The very same God who meets us on the mountaintop walks with us, in the person of our Lord Jesus Christ, into the valley of real life.

On the way down that mountain, Jesus tried to teach them some of the most important lessons they would ever hear. He tried to help them understand the fact that he was headed for a great trial. This lesson was not easy to learn, certainly not as pleasing as the mountaintop, but it would become central to the lives of these disciples. Jesus told them to keep quiet about the experience until after the resurrection—an idea that completely baffled them. So they changed the subject, asking about what the "scribes" (v. 11) said regarding Elijah. Jesus responded by pointing again toward where his mission was headed: "many sufferings" (v. 12).

There was a remarkable change of mood from Peter's ecstasy in verse 6 to the talk of suffering. To make it worse, they were hardly down from the mountain before they were confronted with arguments and accusations between the other disciples and the scribes. Peter may have had it right after all. If only they could have stayed up on that mountain.

Can you hear the lesson for us? Sometimes we think we only really experience the presence of God in those rare, mountaintop moments. But the very same God who meets us on the mountaintop walks with us, in the person of our Lord Jesus Christ, into the valley of real life. As Christ walks with us, he begins to teach us by the indwelling presence of the Holy Spirit. We begin to learn how to apply the lessons of the mountain to the places where we live and work day after day.

Are there some significant mountaintop experiences in your life? Perhaps you've known some moments when God seemed so near, but now life has become rather ordinary again. Perhaps you find yourself longing for one of those mountaintop experiences again. Hear the simple good news of this story in its context: when you come down from the mountaintop, Jesus comes with you. We really need to know this. Otherwise, we can grow cynical about mountaintop experiences. We need mountaintop moments; they are an important part of our spiritual journey. But we also need to realize that God never intended for us to live there all the time. These disciples were marching into some of the darkest days they would ever know. But Jesus was with them, and Jesus is with us by his Spirit, coming alongside us in our valley journeys.

Go to the mountain. Don't be afraid of it, and do not mistrust it. But realize that, when you come down, you don't leave the presence of God. The risen Christ comes with you.

—Jeren Rowell

DAY 19

Additional Scripture Readings:
Psalm 89:1–4, 19–26; 2 Samuel 6:1–11

———

[1] In the past God spoke to our ancestors through the prophets at many times and in various ways, [2] but in these last days he has spoken to us by his Son, whom he appointed heir of all things, and through whom also he made the universe. [3] The Son is the radiance of God's glory and the exact representation of his being, sustaining all things by his powerful word. After he had provided purification for sins, he sat down at the right hand of the Majesty in heaven. [4] So he became as much superior to the angels as the name he has inherited is superior to theirs.

—Hebrews 1:1–4

GOD SPOKE

One of my favorite parts of the Advent season is the Christmas Eve nativity play put on by the children in our church. There are parts for as many children as want to participate, so some years we have ten shepherds or seven wise men or four innkeepers. Come one, come all! Whoever wants a speaking part gets one! They walk to the front of the church, marching right down the center aisle between stained-glass windows that depict the very story they are about to act out. The angel announces Jesus's arrival, Mary sings a lovely song, and even Joseph has a line.

But one character remains conspicuously speechless: the baby Jesus. Now, I know that babies do not talk. But in a play such as this, where children play animals and even the star is personified, it wouldn't surprise me if Jesus were given at least one line: perhaps a word of encouragement to his mother or a simple thank you to the wise men for wandering all that way with such nice gifts.

Still, Jesus says nothing. He lies there in the manger, the center of the universe in that moment, surrounded by his parents and the animals and the visitors, and he doesn't say a single thing. In that moment, Jesus—God—is silent.

Sometimes God feels more quiet during Advent than any other season. The short, cold days are swallowed by the long, dark nights.

Sometimes I look around the world, and it feels like God is still silent. When I see ongoing conflicts waged by men of war, conflicts that take the lives of the innocent and leave families displaced, wandering in the wilderness, I wonder why God doesn't say something. When I hear stories of human beings being trafficked like goods, being used for all purposes and against their will, I wish God would say something. When I walk the long streets of my city and bear witness to the seemingly endless cycle of poverty, much of it caused by injustice and unfair practices, I desperately wish God would say something. "Speak up, God!" I want to cry out.

Sometimes God feels more quiet during Advent than any other season. The short, cold days are swallowed by the long, dark nights. People walk quietly, buried inside their hats and gloves and coats, not saying anything. The saddest parts of our lives seem to come into focus during this season of waiting. "Why are you so silent, God?" But as Christmas draws closer, it is important to remember that our waiting *will* end. On Christmas morning, God speaks. "But in these last days, he has spoken to us by his Son" (Hebrews 1:2).

Imagine the silence of God experienced by the Israelites in the Old Testament, sometimes going generations before once again hearing from God through a prophet. Imagine the questions and doubts they must have had, when all they could do was continue trying to make a living in the wilderness and lean on the stories passed down to them from previous generations.

Imagine the awe that accompanied Paul's letter when he said, "In the past God spoke to our ancestors through the prophets at many times and in various ways, but in these last days he has spoken to us by his Son, whom he appointed heir of all things, and through whom also he made the universe" (vv. 1–2).

God is no longer silent, speaking only by proxy through imperfect men. In these last days, he has spoken through his Son, the "exact representation of his being" (v. 3). In other words, God speaks to us directly, if we will only have ears to hear.

Last year, my three daughters took part in our church's play. My daughter Abra was one of the many innkeepers ("non-speaking part, please, Dad"); my daughter Poppy played the role of baby Jesus, and she did great (as long as baby Jesus was allowed a pacifier); and my daughter Lucy stood in as Mary. The narrators guided the story, and all the children were spectacular. But even as we gathered that night to bear witness to the reliving of the incarnation of Christ, the world pulsed in turmoil: bombs dropped onto Syria, refugees fled for safer shores, and the church in the United States was as divided as ever. It appeared that, once again, God was remaining silent.

Thank goodness not all is as it appears. God has spoken to us through his son, Jesus. May we learn to listen to the voice of the Shepherd.

—Shawn Smucker

DAY 20

Today's Scripture Reading:
Psalm 89:1–4, 19–26

Additional Scripture Readings:
2 Samuel 6:12–19 and Hebrews 1:5–14

---

[1] I will sing of the LORD's great love forever;
with my mouth I will make your
faithfulness known
through all generations.
[2] I will declare that your love stands firm
forever,
that you have established your faithfulness
in heaven itself.
[3] You said, "I have made a covenant with
my chosen one,
I have sworn to David my servant,
[4] 'I will establish your line forever
and make your throne firm through
all generations.'"

[19] Once you spoke in a vision,
to your faithful people you said:
"I have bestowed strength on a warrior;

I have raised up a young man from among
the people.
[20] I have found David my servant;
with my sacred oil I have anointed him.
[21] My hand will sustain him;
surely my arm will strengthen him.
[22] The enemy will not get the better of him;
the wicked will not oppress him.
[23] I will crush his foes before him
and strike down his adversaries.
[24] My faithful love will be with him,
and through my name his horn will be
exalted.
[25] I will set his hand over the sea,
his right hand over the rivers.
[26] He will call out to me, 'You are my
Father,
my God, the Rock my Savior.'"

—Psalm 89:1–4, 19–26

MY CHOSEN ONE

Have you ever found yourself clinging to the promises of God in the middle of a tough situation? Imagine living as a Jewish captive of the Babylonian Empire. For a while, your city was under siege, the noise and destruction possibly all you'd ever known. Finally, your king was tracked down and ripped away, and the city itself fell. Now you've been taken to a hostile foreign country. Your future remains uncertain. What now? How do you sing the songs of your people? Where is God? What does your song sound like in the midst of despair? "How long, Lord? Will you hide yourself forever? How long will your wrath burn like fire?" (Psalm 89:46).

The Jewish people saw Babylonian captivity as the consequence of their service to other gods. The people, especially some of their rulers, had trusted in human strength more than they trusted in the God of their ancestors. And now here they were, far from their homes in the land God had given them. In a way, they had brought this upon themselves. Psalm 89—not a psalm of joy in prosperity but a cry of mourning to the God of the universe—was written in the context of Babylonian captivity. Imagine the tears of the author, stuck in this mess, unsure of the future, singing:

I will sing of the Lord's great love forever;
with my mouth I will make your faithfulness known
through all generations.
I will declare that your love stands firm forever,
that you have established your faithfulness in heaven itself (vv. 1–2).

And then reminding God of the promise to King David long ago:

You said, "I have made a covenant with my chosen one,
I have sworn to David my servant,
'I will establish your line forever
and make your throne firm through all generations'" (vv. 3–4).

In singing Psalm 89, the broken people of God clung to the promise that somehow, even in the midst of their current despair, David's line would someday continue as a sign of God's faithfulness.

But how? The monarchy had failed and, with it, the hope of God's steadfast love and mercy being mediated through David's descendants. The future was hard to see in that moment. Their kingdom was in shambles, and their greatest minds were exiled to faraway Babylon. Yet still they sang of a God whose faithfulness would be known through all generations through the line of David—a love that would stand firm forever. They expected God's love to be mediated through human beings—the descendants of King David.

Maybe you were expecting a trumpet sound or a miracle or a king, but what you will end up with is a bright-hearted teenage girl and a baby in a cold, prickly manger.

At the end of Psalm 89, the writer cried out in lament: "Oh, Lord, where is the unfailing love you showed in times past? And where is the proof of your faithfulness to David?" The answer would come hundreds of years later, in the story of the sudden calling of a nervous teenager named Mary.

Once, when I was studying abroad in Belgium, some Spanish friends of mine convinced me to spend a day with them in Brussels, a French-speaking city more than twenty miles away from our Flemish-speaking town. Later that night, I was unexpectedly separated from the group. With no French skills and only a few euros left, I bought a ticket on a bus I hoped was headed toward the train station. After just a few stops, I realized I had no idea where I was. I was lost! Twenty miles from my apartment and thousands of miles from home, I had no idea what to do next. The last train back to Leuven would be departing soon, but I had no idea how to get to the train station. I literally cried out to God. Tears streaming down my face, I wondered, *Where are you? What do I do now? Help!* I expected a sign from God like a sudden ability to speak French or some other unexpected happening.

Then I heard from the row behind me two girls speaking perfect English. I prayed for the courage to ask them for help. They turned out to be the teenage children of UN ambassadors and the only English speakers I met in that entire city. They had never met a theology student before, and they peppered me with questions about God, Jesus, and the gospel all the way back to the city center. Instead of a disembodied miracle for myself, God chose me to reveal God's faithful love to those two teenagers.

Here's the thing: even when you feel abandoned by God, know that God is still faithful, and God will show up. But here's the other thing: it's probably not going to be when or what you were expecting. Maybe you were expecting a trumpet sound or a miracle or a king, but what you will end up with is a bright-hearted teenage girl and a baby in a cold, prickly manger.

When the angel Gabriel appeared to Mary he declared, "Do not be afraid, Mary; you have found favor with God. You will conceive and give birth to a son, and you are to call him Jesus. He will be great and will be called the Son of the Most High. The Lord God will give him the throne of his father David, and he will reign over Jacob's descendants forever; his kingdom will never end" (Luke 1:30–33). Finally, hundreds of years after the Babylonian captivity, as a sign of the faithfulness of God, she is chosen. Once again, God's love revealed is through a human being.

God was revealed to the world through Jesus. This baby in a manger was a sign of God's unending, faithful love toward God's people. To a people who perhaps still felt abandoned, the coming of the Messiah meant hope and restoration.

God's faithful love is revealed through human beings; you and I are the continuation of this long line of incarnation. Remember this in those moments when you feel abandoned: you are chosen.

—Brit Bolerjack

DAY 21

Today's Scripture Reading:
John 7:40–52

Additional Scripture Readings:
Psalm 89:1–4, 19-26; Judges 13:2–24

---

⁴⁰ On hearing his words, some of the people said, "Surely this man is the Prophet."

⁴¹ Others said, "He is the Messiah."

Still others asked, "How can the Messiah come from Galilee? ⁴² Does not Scripture say that the Messiah will come from David's descendants and from Bethlehem, the town where David lived?" ⁴³ Thus the people were divided because of Jesus. ⁴⁴ Some wanted to seize him, but no one laid a hand on him.

⁴⁵ Finally the temple guards went back to the chief priests and the Pharisees, who asked them, "Why didn't you bring him in?"

⁴⁶ "No one ever spoke the way this man does," the guards replied.

⁴⁷ "You mean he has deceived you also?" the Pharisees retorted. ⁴⁸ "Have any of the rulers or of the Pharisees believed in him? ⁴⁹ No! But this mob that knows nothing of the law—there is a curse on them."

⁵⁰ Nicodemus, who had gone to Jesus earlier and who was one of their own number, asked, ⁵¹ "Does our law condemn a man without first hearing him to find out what he has been doing?"

⁵² They replied, "Are you from Galilee, too? Look into it, and you will find that a prophet does not come out of Galilee."

—John 7:40–52

OUT OF GALILEE

But the voice which reigns, the voice by which we were taught by God himself concerning God, was the voice of Jesus Christ. Along all the path now behind us we could not take a single step without stumbling again and again across that name.

—*Karl Barth*

I am learning to navigate the obstacles of a house that includes a toddler. In a distant memory, my house rests in the tranquil peace of calm and order. Now it has transformed into a volatile minefield littered with the toys of a two-year-old. Sometimes, after bedtime, when the lights have gone out, I try to maneuver around the house. Admittedly, I have made better decisions in my life. It's dangerous out there. I have been forced to watch where I step; otherwise, I may stumble and trip my way through the night.

Nicodemus's stumbling likewise began at night, when the lights went out. Sitting in the dark on top of a flat, Judean roof, Nicodemus encountered a peculiarly talking man. He was from Galilee and said things like, "No one can see the kingdom of God unless they are born again" (John 3:3).

Perplexed, curious, and seeking, Nicodemus asked, "How can someone be born when they are old? Surely they cannot enter a second time into their mother's womb to be born!" (v. 4).

Nicodemus knew there was something different about this teacher, but he couldn't quite place his finger on the peculiarity. Maybe he had heard about the baptism in the Jordan or the wedding at Cana. Perhaps he had been educated on the many signs and miracles of this man, but there was something more—something that was deeply compelling about this man named Jesus. As they sat there in the cool of the night, I imagine Nicodemus stumbling his way through the dark, trying to figure out why he was so compelled by this man.

The scene from today's reading was tense. There was confusion concerning this strange character from Galilee, and party lines had been drawn. Division hung in the air. Was he the Prophet—the one Moses spoke about? Maybe he was the Messiah, coming to save and restore sacred Israel. Could a Messiah come from Galilee?

As keepers of the law, the Pharisees concluded that the long-awaited Messiah could not possibly hail from Galilee and subsequently demanded his arrest. They took pride in their interpretation of the true, hard facts of the law. The law, after all, separated the ignorant from the knowledgeable and the foolish from the wise. The Pharisees employed the temple guards to find and arrest this peculiar Galilean, but when they found him, they too were divided. They couldn't bring themselves to execute the orders. They had never heard anyone speak like Jesus did.

> For all we know, faith might be about learning how to walk in the darkness; learning how to navigate between belief and doubt.

Nicodemus was conflicted too, having first encountered Jesus on a rooftop in the dark. There was something about Jesus that Nicodemus could not forget. Should he go along with the plans of his colleagues to pursue arrest, or should he seek one more night in the presence of Jesus? Risking his reputation and maybe even his life, he drew the Pharisees back to the law, urging them to offer Jesus the opportunity to defend himself before they made up their minds against him. Again, the peculiarity of this Galilean cast doubt on religious certainty and demanded one more conversation.

I wonder if Nicodemus couldn't forget the gentle breeze from their nighttime conversation. Did he remember the brightness of the stars and their radiant glow as he talked with Jesus? I wonder if Nicodemus couldn't escape how he felt meandering in the night as Jesus explained to him the intricacies of faith, trust, and new birth. Something was at work in Nicodemus, causing him to stumble over everything he had ever believed.

Nicodemus's doubt of religious certainty rose in the darkness. For all we know, faith might be about learning how to walk in the darkness; learning how to navigate *between* belief and doubt. And not the type of doubt that leads to unbelief but doubt in the knowledge that says all that can be known *is* known, that law is law, and that a Galilean can't be the Messiah. Perhaps faith rises out of darkness in the cool of the night, in the sensation of sneaking out under the moonlight to sit at the feet of a peculiarly talking man from Galilee speaking about the promise of new life.

In his plea on behalf of Jesus, I wonder if Nicodemus wasn't just scheming for another chance to stand in his presence, to sit at his feet. Was he hoping for one more night on the roof? Did he intend to give his life to receive the compelling man from Galilee? For Nicodemus, there was something intoxicating about this man.

In the light shed by Jesus, Nicodemus stumbled over certainty. Everything was turned upside down. He stumbled over a Galilean voice that called forth new life—not unlike a Creator. He stumbled over a voice that resurrected death—not unlike a voice that could bring life forth out of dust. He stumbled over a peculiar voice in an unlikely place, from an unusual town—a voice that shouldn't belong to the Messiah yet spoke and acted like the God Nicodemus had always known. Like learning to walk in the dark, Nicodemus kept tripping over Jesus. There was just something about him, and it didn't make a lot of sense, but night was becoming day, and Nicodemus was becoming reborn.

During this season of Advent, might Jesus be inviting us to sit in his presence and wrestle between patience and unrest as we wait for the unlikely coming of a Galilean King? Here in our waiting, in the dark, we come to the sense that we are not alone. Christ is with us, having come to meet us in the moments and from the places where we least expect him to be. God is so incarnate, so providential, that we keep stumbling over God's presence time and time again. During this season, may we give ourselves to the peculiar voice that calls in the middle of the night, inviting us to the journey of stumbling again and again over that name that is above all other names—the name of Jesus.

—**Jake Edwards**

"I am the Lord's servant," Mary answered. "May your word to me be fulfilled." Then the angel left her.
—Luke 1:38

She Is Chosen

WEEKLY PRAYER

My soul glorifies the Lord
and my spirit rejoices in God my Savior,
for he has been mindful
of the humble state of his servant.
From now on all generations will call me blessed,
for the Mighty One has done great things for me—
holy is his name.
His mercy extends to those who fear him,
from generation to generation.
He has performed mighty deeds with his arm;
he has scattered those who are proud in their inmost thoughts.
He has brought down rulers from their thrones
but has lifted up the humble.
He has filled the hungry with good things
but has sent the rich away empty.
He has helped his servant Israel,
remembering to be merciful
to Abraham and his descendants forever,
just as he promised our ancestors.

—Luke 1:46b–55

MEMORY VERSE CHALLENGE

But the angel said to her, "Do not be afraid, Mary; you have found favor with God. You will conceive and give birth to a son, and you are to call him Jesus."

—Luke 1:30–31

Come to the Table

Sunday Scripture Reading:
Luke 1:26–38

Additional Scripture Readings:
**2 Samuel 7:1–11, 16; Psalm 89:1–4, 19–26;
Romans 16:25–27**

---

[30] But the angel said to her, "Do not be afraid, Mary; you have found favor with God. [31] You will conceive and give birth to a son, and you are to call him Jesus. [32] He will be great and will be called the Son of the Most High. The Lord God will give him the throne of his father David, [33] and he will reign over Jacob's descendants forever; his kingdom will never end."

—Luke 1:30–33

THE MOTHER OF JESUS

We talk so often about the end—about the inn and the shepherds in their fields and the baah-ing of the sheep drowned out by the cries of a newborn and the triumph of the skies and the choruses of angels. O, holy night.

But before any of this could take place, a young girl from a small town, already betrothed, was chosen. Before there could be a story of an inn without rooms and a baby wrapped in swaddling clothes, there is the story of a simple Jewish girl with callused hands from long days of learning how to run a house, bake the bread, and make the clothing for the family she would soon have.

And there's also the story of the terrifying moment when an angel appeared and her heart quaked—because she knew that the news the angel brought would change her world forever. In every way, large and small, the entire world would change.

Mary was not anything exceptional in her world. She didn't come from a family with social standing or even a notable town. Instead, she was like you, or me. She was only a girl, doing her best to please her family, doing what was expected of her, preparing to marry a carpenter, to keep his house and raise their children.

And yet God chose her. Where the world sees ordinary, God sees a vessel for a plan's fulfillment. Where we see human frailty or fear, God must see the greatest of strength. God did choose her—this young girl from a backwater town who was already betrothed. God chose her to carry the Son.

How frightening and awesome to be such a vessel, called by God, to do what sounds impossible, to boldly defy logic, cultural norms, and everything else you've lived up to your whole life. But that was exactly what young—nothing-exceptional, ordinary-as-homemade-clothing, dirt-under-her-fingernails, tremors-of-uncertainty-in-her-heart—Mary, did.

And the rest—is history.

—Melanie Haney

QUESTIONS FOR DISCUSSION OR REFLECTION

Has there ever been a time when you didn't feel worthy of something? What did it feel like to receive something undeserved?

What do you think it must have felt like to be Mary that evening when the angel visited?

On the eve of Jesus's birth, how can we celebrate being chosen by Jesus?

FAMILY TIME

Together with your family, look at your Christmas tree, or look at pictures of different Christmas trees decorated for the season. Invite each person to point out a favorite ornament. Discuss how the ornaments bring extraordinary beauty to something that would otherwise be quite ordinary.

In the same way, Mary was an ordinary girl whom God used to bring extraordinary peace, beauty, salvation, and redemption to the world.

Discuss some practical ways you can allow God to use your family to help others. Write these ideas down on strips of paper and make them into a paper-chain garland to hang on your Christmas tree or elsewhere in your home. When you take down your Christmas decorations, look again at these ideas and commit to doing one, some, or all of them over the course of the next year.

Glory to God in the highest heaven,
and on earth peace to those on
whom his favor rests.
—Luke 2:14

CHRISTMAS DAY

He Is Here

CHRISTMAS HYMN

Joy to the world! The Lord is come.
Let earth receive her King;
Let every heart prepare him room,
And heaven and nature sing,
And heaven and nature sing,
And heaven, and heaven and nature sing.

Joy to the world! The Savior reigns!
Let men their songs employ;
While fields and floods, rocks, hills, and plains
Repeat the sounding joy,
Repeat the sounding joy,
Repeat, repeat the sounding joy.

No more let sins and sorrow grow,
Nor thorns infest the ground;
He comes to make his blessings flow
Far as the curse is found,
Far as the curse is found,
Far as, far as the curse is found.

He rules the world with truth and grace,
And makes the nations prove
The glories of his righteousness,
And wonders of his love,
And wonders of his love,
And wonders, wonders of his love.

—Isaac Watts

Come to the Table

Sunday Scripture Reading:
Luke 2:1–20

THE BIRTH OF JESUS AS TOLD IN LUKE 2:1-20

[1] In those days Caesar Augustus issued a decree that a census should be taken of the entire Roman world. [2] (This was the first census that took place while Quirinius was governor of Syria.) [3] And everyone went to their own town to register.

[4] So Joseph also went up from the town of Nazareth in Galilee to Judea, to Bethlehem the town of David, because he belonged to the house and line of David. [5] He went there to register with Mary, who was pledged to be married to him and was expecting a child. [6] While they were there, the time came for the baby to be born, [7] and she gave birth to her firstborn, a son. She wrapped him in cloths and placed him in a manger, because there was no guest room available for them.

[8] And there were shepherds living out in the fields nearby, keeping watch over their flocks at night. [9] An angel of the Lord appeared to them, and the glory of the Lord shone around them, and they were terrified. [10] But the angel said to them, "Do not be afraid. I bring you good news that will cause great joy for all the people. [11] Today in the town of David a Savior has been born to you; he is the Messiah, the Lord. [12] This will be a sign to you: You will find a baby wrapped in cloths and lying in a manger."

[13] Suddenly a great company of the heavenly host appeared with the angel, praising God and saying,

[14] "Glory to God in the highest heaven,
and on earth peace to those on whom his favor rests."

[15] When the angels had left them and gone into heaven, the shepherds said to one another, "Let's go to Bethlehem and see this thing that has happened, which the Lord has told us about."

[16] So they hurried off and found Mary and Joseph, and the baby, who was lying in the manger. [17] When they had seen him, they spread the word concerning what had been told them about this child, [18] and all who heard it were amazed at what the shepherds said to them. [19] But Mary treasured up all these things and pondered them in her heart. [20] The shepherds returned, glorifying and praising God for all the things they had heard and seen, which were just as they had been told.

FAMILY TIME

In the busyness of Christmas Day, take a moment to gather as a family around the table or around a manger scene and read Luke 2:1–20 aloud. Then pray the following Christmas prayer together.

CHRISTMAS PRAYER

Jesus, today as we remember your birth, we give you glory. Thank you for bringing peace to our lives. We can't wait to see the things you will do through our family. Use us to show your love to those around us.

BRIT BOLERJACK
*College & Community
Pastor, Oklahoma City
First Church of the
Nazarene; Director,
Young Clergy Network*

DANA BOWMAN
Author and Blogger

ROBBIE CANSLER
*Lead Pastor, The Mission
Church of the Nazarene*

JAKE EDWARDS
*Lead Pastor, New
Beginnings Church
of the Nazarene*

MARK FULLER
*Lead Pastor, Grove City
Church of the Nazarene*

**SHAWNA SONGER
GAINES**
*Chaplain, Trevecca
Nazarene University*

TIMOTHY R. GAINES
*Assistant Professor
of Religion, Trevecca
Nazarene University*

MELANIE HANEY
Writer and Blogger

DEANNA HAYDEN
*Lead Pastor, Southwood
Church of the Nazarene*

BROOKLYN LINDSEY
Global Justice Advocate,
Church of the Nazarene

JASON MCPHERSON
Lead Pastor, Journey
Church of the Nazarene

RACHEL MCPHERSON
Curator, The Foundry
Community Blog

JESSE MIDDENDORF
General Superintendent
Emeritus, Church of the
Nazarene; Founder and
Executive Director, Center
for Pastoral Leadership

MICHAEL R. PALMER
Lead Pastor, Living Vine
Church of the Nazarene

BRETT RICKEY
Lead Pastor,
Highland Park Church
of the Nazarene

JEREN ROWELL
Superintendent, Kansas
City District Church
of the Nazarene

SHAWN SMUCKER
Author and Blogger

CARLA SUNBERG
General Superintendent,
Church of the Nazarene